WEIRD CANADIAN PLACES

Humorous, Bizarre, Peculiar & Strange
Locations & Attractions across the Nation

Dan de Figueiredo

**BLUE
BIKE
BOOKS**

The Publisher: Blue Bike Books

Library and Archives Canada Cataloguing in Publication

De Figueiredo, Dan, 1964–
  Weird Canadian places: humorous, bizarre, peculiar and strange locations and attractions across the nation / Dan de Figueiredo.

ISBN-13: 978-0-9739116-4-0
ISBN-10: 0-9739116-4-6

  1. Canada—Miscellanea. 2. Canada—Description and travel—Miscellanea. I. Title.

FC60.D26 2006   971   C2006-901646-1

Project Director: Nicholle Carrière
Project Editor: Nicholle Carrière
Illustrations: Roger Garcia
Cover Image: Roger Garcia

PC: P5

CONTENTS

INTRODUCTION 6

UNDERGROUND AND OVERHEAD 10

GRUESOME AND GHOULISH 29
The Gruesome 30
And Now...the Ghoulish 34

HAUNTED HOMES, HOSTELS AND THEATRES 44

NATURE'S SO NUTTY 56

IT'S A GHOST WHAT? A PHANTOM WHO? 74
Places Where the Ghosts Tend to Float 75
Places Where the Ghosts Ride 81
Places Where Ghosts Frolic in the Great Outdoors 86

LAKES AND BAYS AND THEIR SOGGY INHABITANTS . 95

INTERPLANETARY KRAFT, NEITHER ORANGE NOR
INDIVIDUALLY WRAPPED 110
Places to Have Fun with UFOs 113
Places for the Serious UFO Nut 118

ODD, MYSTERIOUS OR ON THE VERGE OF BEING
OFFENSIVE 123
The Odd 125
The Mysterious 134
Definitely on the Verge of Being Offensive 136

IF I CAN CELEBRATE THERE, I CAN CELEBRATE
ANYWHERE 138

A CRATER, A RING OR A GLOWING ORB 158

IT'S NOT OVER! 167

DEDICATION

This book is dedicated to the oh so many people who have let me be part of their lives and in some way nurtured any talent I might possess. To my mother, Sharon Lindsay, and my grandmother, Sarah Tilbury, for passing down the strength and ability to see beyond the hype that allowed me to take up the life of a writer and be "poor." Right, mum? To my Uncle Brian and Aunt Dawn for giving me a copy of Robinson Crusoe—I know that book started me on this path. To my mother-in-law, Gena Figueiredo, thank you for your openness, your *bacalhau* and all the laughter. To Max, for being my constant companion for more than 10 years. Sorry about the peeing, but I bet the boiled chicken is better than ever. To the three most important male influences in my life—Bob, Simon and Paulo—thank you for inspiring me to be better. And, I suppose, most of all, I must thank God for toying with my emotions, pulling the rug out from under me and never letting me get too full of myself. I've learned my lesson. I really don't think I'm the smartest person in the room. Not all the time, anyway. Thank God for those "gotcha moments" and for making my life a journey. You have some weird sense of humour!

ACKNOWLEDGEMENTS

This book could not have been written without the generous help of a great many "weird" Canadians. First, I have to thank my publisher who took a chance and let me write this book. I have had the best time researching, writing and putting this together. I also have to thank my editor, Nicholle Carrière. Having worked much of my professional career as an editor, I know that a good editor can make or break the final product.

I also have to thank a great many people from the various government tourist offices, town's, sights, festivals etc. If I've forgotten anyone, I do apologize. But here is a list of people whose help was invaluable. They include: Paul Figueiredo; Sharon Lindsay; John Fisher; Bill Lishman; Jane Sims; Gillian Marx, Market Development Officer, Media Relations, Newfoundland and Labrador Tourism; R. Randy Brooks, Manager, Media Relations, Nova Scotia

Department of Tourism, Culture and Heritage; John Marr, Waterfront Visitor Information Centre, Nova Scotia; Bernadette MacNeil, Destination Cape Breton Association; Carol Horne, Manager, Advertising and Publicity, Tourism PEI; Donna Rowley, Manager, Prince Edward Island Potato Museum; Diane Rioux, Media Relations-Tourism, Tourism and Parks, Tourism New Brunswick; Isabel Gil, Director Destination Québec/Tourisme Québec; Magalie Boutin, Destination Québec/Tourism Québec; Sophie Saint-Gelais, Agente de promotion touristique, Ville de Baie-Comeau; Ontario Tourism Marketing Partnership; Bev Carret, Manager, Government and Community Relations, Art Gallery of Ontario; Eunice Henning (the Big Adirondack Chairs); Daryl Demoskoff, Media Relations Coordinator, Tourism Saskatchewan; The Town of Wilkie, Saskatchewan; Harold Wasylenka of Wynyard, Saskatchewan (my Chicken Chariot race source); Rollie Bourassa, Regina, Saskatchewan (the Pemmican Pete insider); Marilyn at Danceland, Manitou Beach, Saskatchewan; Susan Fekete, Travel Media Relations Specialist, Americas, Travel Alberta International; Becky Fox, Coordinator, Information Services, Vulcan Tourism and Trek Station, Vulcan, Alberta; Carla Mont, Tourism BC; Brenda from HelloBC.com; Heidi Korven, Administrative Assistant, Kootenay Rockies Tourism; Miles Prodan, Director of Communications and Marketing, Thompson Okanagan Tourism Association; John Bass, Media Relations Coordinator, Northern British Columbia Tourism Association; Lana Kingston, Media Relations Manager, Tourism Vancouver Island; Kristine George, Manager, Travel Media Relations (Canada and Overseas), Tourism Victoria; Jeannie McLarnon, Travel Counsellor, Yukon Tourism and Culture; D'Arcy Butler, Marketing and Promotions Manager, Klondike Visitors Association; Samantha Cayen, Administrative Assistant, Klondike Visitors Association; Jennifer Horton, Northwest Territories Tourism; His Royal Highness SnowKing, www.snowking.ca; Brian Webb, Acting Director of Marketing, Nunavut Tourism.

I thank all of these people for their directions, clarifications, redirections, fact-checking and all-around assistance with this weird little book. I hope to run into some of you on my future travels.

INTRODUCTION

"Weird," to me, means odd, unique, interesting, out of the ordinary, not mundane and also fun! It can include the mystical, the paranormal and the unexplained. It includes things described as queer, incomprehensible and mysterious. It can be connected with fate, warning or just plain size. It's a word that can include a great many and varied things.

The question "why" is at the heart of "weird." Why does a headless brakeman roam the former CPR tracks in Vancouver? Why does Lumsden, Saskatchewan, hold an annual Duck Derby? Why does Father Goose live underground and build a replica of Stonehenge out of crushed cars? The answer to "why" defines the weirdness.

Weird does not, in my mind, have a bad connotation, though I do accept that many people got weirded out when I called them and said I was writing a book on weird Canadian places and wanted to include their place. I heard a lot of silence or the oft-repeated response: "This place isn't weird!" The protest response was all about not wanting to be ridiculed or made fun of. For some reason, the first place people go to when they hear the adjective "weird" is a bad place. Not me. I understand that no one wants to be laughed at, especially by a smarmy citified writer from Toronto. I hope I am not that. My intention is to highlight all the unique places that are everywhere in this country and do it in a lighthearted manner.

In my other life, I occasionally work in television. Please don't hold that against me, though I do not blame you if you do. Last year I had the opportunity to pitch a couple of show ideas to a room full of television executives at the Banff Television Festival. I pitched a paranormal idea that received a warm response. The second idea I pitched involved con games. The response I got from the executives (German TV,

FOX TV, Global TV) was "weird." They called it "weird"! No one thought the paranormal idea was weird, but they all said my con game idea was weird. I took this as a great compliment and a bit of a commentary about television executives—sheep dressed in Armani! I recount this story because I really do think being called weird is a compliment, and I hope that all the places that I've chosen for this book will also accept the "weird" moniker as a great compliment. Heck, why not include it on your town sign: "One of the Weird Places included in the book *Weird Canadian Places*."

My angle of attack in writing the book was to use humour, because other such books I've read like this are…a bit dry. They are well researched, thorough and detailed, but they are encyclopaedic in nature. You'll notice that my tongue is firmly planted in my cheek as I write about each and every one of my weird finds. My intention was to play with all the weirdness that is Canada, not to offend, and I hope everyone who reads this book will take my observations, questions, extrapolations and wit with the intention with which I wrote it. I really hope that you will be entertained. If you learn a little something, that's okay, too.

I structured the book by subject as opposed to compiling a straight province-by-province and location-by-location list. I did this to again avoid the encyclopedic effect that I'm not keen on, but also to show the interesting similarities and differences in weirdness across the country. We are all not as different as we sometimes think.

One of the things that I've discovered about all of us from sea to sea to sea is that we don't take ourselves too seriously. Or if we do, we move to the United States, renounce our citizenship and "are currently under investigation." My research has afforded me the opportunity to learn a great deal about some great places. I have to say that I think Alberta and Saskatchewan "get it"! They, along with New Brunswick, have embraced all that is weird in their parts of the world. They can laugh at it, have fun with it and bring tourists in and not just take their money, but also show them a great time!

There are so many places I now want to visit, though a few months ago I might not have thought so. I am fascinated by the paranormal, intrigued by the oddities that nature has to offer and celebrate all that is kitschy. I'd love to see a ghost train or a fire ship. I have actually seen a UFO, but I don't want to hold myself up for ridicule, so I won't go into that… Okay, I was nine years old, there were all these flashing lights; yes, it might have been an emergency vehicle, but I don't think so. Ambulances, fire trucks and police cars don't hover! Oh, and when I was five years old and living in Woodstock, Ontario, I thought the abandoned drum of an old cement mixer was actually a three-man splashdown capsule that NASA had left out behind my house. The eyes of a child! I turned a mundane old cement-mixing drum into a spaceship. Weird! That's the kind of weird that this book is about.

The choices I've made are, indeed, arbitrary. My interpretation of what is interesting, odd and weird is probably different from what many other people in the world would designate as weird. However, I'm the one who wrote the book, so enjoy it or go write your own… Seriously, there were so many weird places that I don't think I've even covered a quarter of them, and I suspect that the number will just continue to grow. Who knows, maybe there'll be a *Weird Canadian Places, Volume 2*.

There may be a great many weird Canadian "things" that I have omitted. However, the parameters of this book were specific to weird "places." Some weird things crossed over and could be directly pegged to place. A great many of the weirdest things do not lend themselves to this type of specificity, so they got tossed. I also tended to avoid places considered weird just because of their place names. There are enough of these in Newfoundland alone to fill a full volume. Those weird places that made it to final cut tend to be current, ongoing and recurring sites of weirdness. In general, I avoided one-offs, lone occurrences and, except in a very few instances, weird places that are only weird because of something that happened in the past.

Peppered throughout the book you will read all about the various "Big, Gargantuan & Ridiculously Oversized" things that have been foisted upon the Canadian landscape. There are a lot of "world's biggest" in this vast land of ours. Some might suggest it screams of a national inferiority complex. However, I choose to look at it differently and applaud all those ambitious little communities that have figured out how to get tourists to their "little piece of heaven." Whether that's to see the "World's Biggest Inukshuk" or "Mac the Moose," who cares! If you build it big in Canada, tourists will come a-runnin' with cameras in hand…

Embrace the weirdness!

Dan de Figueiredo

Underground
and Overhead

In this chapter, we look at the weirdest places you'd never be able to spot and those you can't possibly miss—the little hidden gems literally beneath the ground and others that are not only out in the open but scream "Look at me!"

It's monstrosities vs. little hidden wonders; odd architecture vs. Cold War bunker; mysterious lost mine vs. money pit; haunted tunnel vs. escape tunnel

You get the idea.
Here are Canada's underground wonders and aboveground screamers.

THE DIEFENBUNKER
CARP, ONTARIO

The promotional literature asks the question: "Looking for a different site for your tours to visit?" Well, you've definitely found it here. The Diefenbunker, as it is affectionately called, is one of those Cold War relics you'd think could only be found in the United States or Russia. But no, the Diefenbunker is real and is located just 35 kilometres east of Ottawa in the community of Carp...or more accurately, underneath the community of Carp.

The Diefenbunker was built between 1959 and 1961 and was intended to house essential government and military personnel in case of a nuclear attack. It's a four-storey facility built into a hill and is designed to survive a five-megaton blast a kilometre and a half away. Although the idea of such a Cold War relic serving as a Cold War museum is kitschy, to say the least, the Historic Sites and Monuments Board of Canada has called the Diefenbunker "the most important surviving Cold War site in Canada." And it almost didn't survive.

When Canadian Forces Station Carp (the official name of the Diefenbunker) was closed in 1994, the government gutted the facility. Some of its original artifacts were dispersed to the Canadian War Museum, the Canadian Museum of Civilization and the Military Communications and Electronics Museum in Kingston, but most of the contents disappeared for good. However, the museum's staff has done an amazing job of begging, borrowing and stealing (not literally) original artifacts and recreating others to fill the Diefenbunker and give it a real sense of its Cold War–era prime.

A 90-minute tour through the meandering facility takes visitors through a time warp into the 1960s. Visitors experience the blast tunnel, the air lock, the top-level hallway, the Federal Warning Centre, the machine room, the CBC Radio studio, the Bank of Canada vault, the War Cabinet room and the prime minister's suite and offices.

And I'll bet that in the cramped prime minister's quarters you can well imagine Prime Minister John Diefenbaker, with his jowls a-flappin', practising his bad French while commanding Canada's response to a nuclear attack (which I believe consisted of officially sitting and waiting to see what the Americans would do). For a weird and wacky blast from the past, the Diefenbunker is high on our list of special places.

THE TUNNELS OF MOOSE JAW
MOOSE JAW, SASKATCHEWAN

The town of Moose Jaw has one of Canada's weirdest tourist attractions—tunnels. That's right, tunnels! Apparently when Moose Jaw's downtown business district was originally con- structed in the late 1800s and early 1900s, passageways were built that ran from the CPR station, under Manitoba Street and to the Maple Leaf Hotel (now called Brewster's) and from there under Main Street to the CER Restaurant (now called Capone's).

Although the locals don't know for sure why these passageways exist, it's thought they were built as utility tunnels. They allowed steam engineers easy access from building to building to main- tain the town's boilers.

What's left of the tunnels includes basement rooms and inter- connected utility corridors. Stories of bootleggers such as Al Capone using the tunnels for escape purposes and other illegal activities are rife in the town.

The "Tunnels of Moose Jaw" tour operator runs two interactive tunnel tours during which tourists become part of the experi- ence while travelling beneath Moose Jaw. Visitors are apparently treated to "state of the art animatronic characters," a multimedia presentation and character tour guides.

The "Chicago Connection" tour explores Chicago's bootlegging connection to Moose Jaw and allows visitors to "lie low" with Al Capone himself. Participants get to be bootleggers who are in town to learn the ropes and buy booze from the Capone organization, all the while staying ahead of the Moose Jaw police. What fun!

The "Passage to Fortune" tour explores the early Chinese immigrant experience, which apparently involved hiding from authorities in the tunnels. This one includes visitors becoming "coolies," working at Burrows and Sons Laundry and ending up in Mr. Wong's Café. I guess with this one, you can experience turn-of-the-century prairie racism at its finest.

The tunnels of Moose Jaw are definitely an underground gem!

THE OAK ISLAND MONEY PIT
OAK ISLAND, NOVA SCOTIA

This may qualify as the weirdest place in Canada because of its strange, enduring, as-yet-unsolved mystery. Oak Island is a small island (57 hectares) in Mahone Bay, on Nova Scotia's eastern shore. Since 1795, people have been intrigued by, focused on and digging at a spot on this island where they think they're going to find some form of buried treasure.

Legend has it that Oak Island won't give up its treasure until its last oak tree has fallen. Which begs the obvious question, why not just cut down all the oak trees and then have at it? I can find no explanation for the wilful flouting of this obvious solution, but there must be some weird treasure hunters' code that forbids it…or in this day and age, provincial legislation against the wilful destruction of oak trees. Whatever.

As the story goes, in 1795, a teenager named Daniel McGinnis tripped over a "curious" circular depression in the ground that just happened to be underneath a tree with cut branches that looked like they'd been used as a pulley. Different place, different time, different type of teenager, I guess, because I have no idea what a branch used as a pulley would look like. Anyway, the enterprising young lad brought two friends on board, and they started digging, all the while with thoughts of Captain Kidd's treasure dancing in their collective heads.

Less than a metre below the surface, they hit flagstones. They became more excited, but found nothing immediately underneath. So they continued digging. At 3 metres down, they hit a layer of oak logs. Underneath that, more dirt… At depths of 6 metres and 9 metres, they hit logs again, but still no treasure. And 9 metres down was as far as they could go on their own. Eight years later, they came back to the money pit along with the Onslow Company and resumed their excavation. They found more and more logs and dirt at regular intervals.

At 27 metres below the surface, they found a stone inscribed with mysterious writing. They pulled that up, along with more oak logs and then the *agua* hit the pit. That's right, the designers of the pit had built an ingenious booby trap that flooded the pit with seawater. *Dios mío!*

Anyway, the boys never did find their treasure. And no one else has been able to get to it either. Attempt after attempt, failure after failure, and at least six deaths directly or indirectly attributed to the pit. And yet people don't give up. Modern technology has been no help either. Except in the area of spreading rumour, innuendo and far-fetched theories on who designed the pit and what the treasure might be. Theories on the pit's builders range from Egyptians, Mayans, Freemasons, Sir Francis Bacon, William Phips, the British, the Knights Templar, Captain Kidd, Blackbeard and the Vikings. Ideas about the treasure range from gold doubloons and pieces of eight to the Holy Grail.

So, if you're in the vicinity of Oak Island… I wouldn't advise digging your own hole, since the place is private property, and in 1985 when I was there, I was chased across the causeway (not really).

In 1995, the Woods Hole Oceanographic Institute (you may remember them from Titanic finding and Bob Ballard fame) was brought in to give their opinion on whether there is something valuable in the pit. Their report is confidential, but rumblings from people who have apparently seen the report say its conclusions are "not discouraging." I wonder if they used the mini sub to come to this underwhelmingly positive conclusion?

Oak Island is currently up for sale with a price tag of $7 million. The Oak Island Tourism Society is calling on various levels of government to purchase the island—pit unseen—and exploit its potential to the fullest. Now that's all we need, government involvement in a pit already known to be a money sucker!

THE LOST LEMON MINE
CROWSNEST PASS, ALBERTA

According to legend, "there's gold in them thar' hills" and murder, mystery, mayhem and a curse! Ewooooewww! In around 1870, as the story goes, a group of American prospectors came to Canada and started panning for gold along the North Saskatchewan River. Two of the prospectors, Frank Lemon and a second man named Blackjack (not to be confused with Yosemite Sam's cartoon character buddy, Black Jack Shellac—they're totally different fellas).

Anyway, Lemon and Blackjack struck out on their own and somehow stumbled across the motherlode of gold mines somewhere near the Crowsnest Pass. The evening of their big score turned from celebration to tragedy when Lemon ended up hacking Blackjack to death with an axe. Distraught, Lemon did the only thing he could and blamed it on Natives, who in turn may or may not have placed a curse on the whole sordid Lemon mining endeavour. Is this all sounding just a bit like that Bogart film, *Treasure of the Sierra Madre*?

Over the next bunch of years, Lemon tried to lead others back to the site of the mine, but whenever he got close, he seemed to go a bit nuts. Others too have tried, but with no luck. A man named McDougall, who was originally dispatched to bury Blackjack, drank himself to death. Another man, Lafayette French, may have found the mine, but he died when his cabin burned down around him. All this gave rise to the legend and curse surrounding the Lost Lemon Mine.

In the 1980s, a man named Ron Stewart claimed to have found the mine, but despite reports by the CBC, the mine turned out to be a pretty crappy gold strike—definitely not up to the calibre of the Lost Lemon's hype.

People continue to try and find the Lost Lemon Mine. Nobody has, but it's given Alberta a great little story about greed and gold and curses. Yeehaw!

~ Big, Gargantuan & Ridiculously Oversized ~

The "World's Largest Blueberry" is located at an Irving Gas Station in Oxford, Nova Scotia (northeast of Springhill). Oxford also claims to be the "Blueberry Capital of the World," so the giant blueberry does make sense. The blueberry is 2.4 metres tall and will take on all challengers!

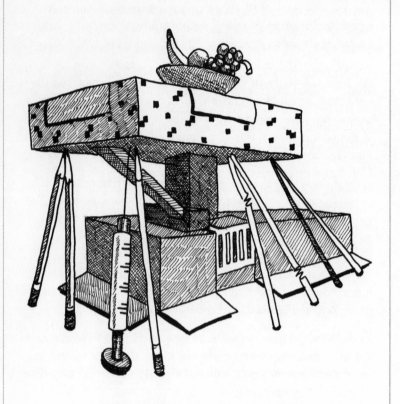

ONTARIO COLLEGE OF ART AND DESIGN
TORONTO, ONTARIO

The "Tabletop" at the Ontario College of Art and Design is one of the strangest additions to any building in a city quickly becoming known for strange additions to buildings. The Sharp Centre for Design, as it is officially known, was designed by British architect Will Alsop and looks as though a child's black-and-white checkerboard pencil box has been precariously balanced atop 12 multicoloured pencils. And yet it's all just an illusion—a little magic mixed with some architectural wonder.

The black-and-white box is actually a conventional two-storey structure that provides classroom and studio space and is held up by the elevator's central core (if you care about engineering).

The Tabletop rests 26 metres in the air and allows great views of Toronto's downtown and the Grange Park, which it shares with the Art Gallery of Ontario. From dusk until midnight, 16 blue metal-halide lights illuminate the Tabletop, giving it a totally different look from its daytime configuration.

Unfortunately there are no public tours of the Sharp Centre. However, it is best viewed from the street where one can't help but be enthralled by its charm. Kitschy, bright, odd, unique and wonderful, the Sharp Centre is everything an addition to a college of art should be! This is one weird building that definitely screams, "Look at me!"

~ Big, Gargantuan & Ridiculously Oversized ~

The "World's Largest Permanent Historical Photo-Mosaic" (now that's a mouthful) covers the sides of a building in Port Carling in Ontario's Muskoka region. Thousands of historical postcards dating back to 1860 were arranged to create a scene 34 metres wide by 14 metres tall, showing a boat on a Muskoka Lake. If you look closely, you can actually see Kurt Russell and Goldie Hawn fighting off the paparazzi on the shore behind the boat. Not really.

THE ART GALLERY OF ONTARIO (AGO)
TORONTO, ONTARIO

Weird is something people have come to expect from world-renowned architect Frank Gehry… And his offer to the city in which he was born, while not quite as weird and wild as the undulating titanium structure in Bilbao, Spain, is nevertheless odd! It has all the hallmarks of becoming as inspirationally famous as Bilbao—it has garnered praise, been heavily criticized and caused both disdain and out and out glee!

The promotional material screams: "Transformation AGO is the vision of a new kind of art museum." One with eyelashes, a sneeze guard or a fallen eyebrow, we would suggest. What am I talking about? Well, the entire north façade rises 21 metres above street level and is 183 metres long. There are two cuts at the east and west extremities of the façade, which makes it look as if it has two eyelashes that are raised high and about to flutter shut. The PR person at the AGO compares them more to wings. Ohhhhhhhh!

Nevertheless, the centre portion of the front façade includes a 137-metre-long promenade on the second floor that allows visitors to look out onto traffic and streetcars on heavily congested Dundas Street, or affords those in their cars or on the streetcar to look inside the AGO while stuck in gridlock. This truly is an example of a museum "giving back." And when you look at the central structure of glass and Douglas fir, you can't help but think salad bar sneeze guard. And when you put the whole façade together and in context, it looks a lot like a Picasso-esque version of a fallen eyebrow…or so we think. We also think it is truly odd, wackily weird and positively wonderful.

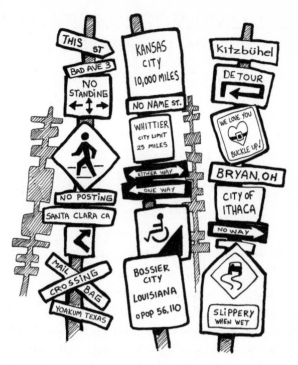

~ Big, Gargantuan & Ridiculously Oversized ~

The town of Watson Lake, Yukon, is located on the Alaska
Highway in the southeastern corner of the territory. Watson
Lake's best-known attraction is the "Signpost Forest." That's
right—a forest made up of signposts. (Didn't they do this on
M*A*S*H?) Located next to the Watson Lake Visitor Information
Centre, the Signpost Forest was started in 1942 by a homesick
U.S. Army G.I. who was working on the construction of the Alaska
Highway. He erected a sign pointing the way to his hometown of
Danville, Illinois, and giving the estimated mileage to get there. It
wasn't long before sheep in the form of people without an original idea of their own followed suit and added their own signs. In
fact, in July 1990, an American couple added the 10,000th sign to
the forest—Bryan, Ohio. So, if you're heading to the Yukon, why
not stop in at Watson Lake and add your hometown's sign. I'd call
first, though. At 10,000 and counting, I'd hate to see you travel all
that way and not be able to mount your sign.

ROYAL ONTARIO MUSEUM (ROM)
TORONTO, ONTARIO

Weird Toronto building number three is, we regret to say, our least favourite. It's definitely monumental, definitely costly and definitely big—it's also overhead and weird. But it looks way too much like it was ill conceived and hastily constructed by Homer Simpson, and when it didn't fit the rest of the building, he crammed it onto the Bloor Street side, where maybe people wouldn't notice. "D-oh!" Does that sound harsh?

Let me start again. Since 1914, the Royal Ontario Museum has been thrilling adults and school groups alike with its dinosaurs, exhibits of natural and cultural history and a really big totem pole (for those of us in Ontario, it's really big).

From the beginning, the ROM buildings themselves were an amalgamation of various architectural influences. So, when it was announced that Daniel Libeskind's crystal-inspired design was going to be added to the north side, it was no great surprise. However, Libeskind's original design involved a lot of glass and a lot of light. The revised design involves a lot less glass, a lot less light and a whole bunch of corrugated metal cladding that screams "suburban backyard." This is not a criticism of suburban backyards. A corrugated metal shed fits there perfectly. I can't imagine a better place for it. But as an addition to one of our country's important cultural institutions, it seems, at best, out of place.

I have, of course, short-changed the Libeskind shed design in one respect. It's not just a square box. In fact, it's a bunch of boxes piled on top of one another, so you couldn't get a right angle if you tried. And that makes it weird!

THE LISHMAN HOUSE
BLACKSTOCK, ONTARIO

How does a home that was featured in magazines such as *Harrowsmith* and *Canadian Architect* as well as on the CBC-TV show *Life and Times* qualify as underground and weird? Well, the "hole" thing has to do with its designer, builder and occupant, Bill Lishman. You could even say that this home transformed its designer from igloo enthusiast to mole man.

That's because Bill Lishman's home is a series of eight interconnected, igloo-like domes that were built with wire-mesh frames, covered with concrete and a bunch of waterproofing materials and then covered over with dirt. A 1970s igloo was Lishman's original inspiration for the structure.

The home features in-floor heating, overhead skylights and a roof that requires mowing. The whole unique structure reminds one of the dwelling in which Luke Skywalker grew up. You know, the one owned by Uncle Owen and Aunt Beru. There isn't a right angle in the entire structure. Arched doorways were hand-made, as was the furniture inside the home. Even the refrigerator is round. It pops out of the kitchen counter at the touch of a button, just like in the 1996 film *Fly Away Home*. Which is no great surprise since that film, about a man who taught geese to fly behind an ultralight plane, is based on the life of our home's designer, Bill Lishman.

KAY-NAH-CHI-WAH-NUNG (MANITOU MOUNDS)
STRATTON, ONTARIO

Kay-Nah-Chi-Wah-Nung ("Place of the Long Rapids") near Rainy River, Ontario, is the site of some of the most interesting underground archaeological digs in the country. As the press information says: "Kay-Nah-Chi-Wah-Nung and the surrounding lands hold the record of almost 8000 years. The Place of the Long Rapids contains the largest group of burial mounds and associated village sites in Canada."

And just what are these mounds and why are they so significant? The mounds are essentially a burial place. The Laurel Culture (300 BC–1100 AD) is thought to be the first group of First Nations people to have built mounds at this site. The Laurel mounds are up to 7 metres high and 18 to 24 metres in diameter. The mound builders would dig a shallow pit, place the deceased inside and cover the remains with earth. Over hundreds of years, more deceased were placed on top and covered with earth. The layering process created the mounds as they are seen today. Sometimes the deceased were buried with medicine bags, pipes, food, clay pots and tools they used in life and would need in death.

The Manitou Mounds site includes a visitor centre that explores the site as a ceremonial centre, its context within North America and the culture of the Ojibway peoples. It's a fascinating look back into the past of First Nations peoples and their burial rituals.

THE PHANTOM SUBWAY STATION
TORONTO, ONTARIO

Myth, folklore, urban legend or reality—that's what people have been asking for decades about the notorious phantom subway station known as Lower Bay. Well, I am happy to tell all that the phantom station does, in fact, exist. This will come as no surprise to older folks who were around when the station was actually used in 1966. So, how was it used, why isn't used anymore and how has the myth surrounding it grown? Hold your horses—I'm getting to it!

So as not to bore those who don't give a flip about Toronto's subway, I'll keep it short. Basically, when the Bloor–Danforth subway line opened in 1966, the Lower Bay Station was a transfer point between the University Line (Lower Bay) and the Bloor–Danforth Line (Upper Bay) in a similar way that the two lines cross at St. George.

The station was also designed and connected by a "phantom tunnel" to Museum Station, just like the one that connects Museum and St. George on the Spadina Line. The three stations formed a "Y" configuration with the purpose that every second train heading north on the University Line could take the right "Y" leg through Lower Bay, and would then connect to the Bloor–Danforth Line before it got to Bloor Station.

The system ran this way for six months, but the configuration was abandoned because it was confusing for passengers. Also, because the whole subway system was interconnected, a single problem anywhere on either subway line disabled the entire system instead of just one line, as it does now.

So Lower Bay was abandoned, and the myth of the phantom station grew. The station is still accessible from Upper Bay by those who have a key. Much of the time, it is used by film companies to shoot creepy subway scenes, which is probably where the myth about it being haunted arose. There are also stories of people who have travelled the "phantom tunnel" to get to Lower Bay, but it is ill advised since it is a dangerous route.

A second "phantom station," which is more like a roughed-in underground streetcar stop, exists at Lower Queen (Yonge and Queen). There are, however, no official documents about a third phantom station at Lower Osgoode.

THE SCREAMING TUNNEL
NIAGARA REGION, ONTARIO

This one falls under the heading of underground and creepily weird! The tunnel in question is not far from Queen Elizabeth Way on Warner Road near Garner Road. I've been there, and the tunnel is dark and smells of sulphur, not to mention that it's often full of water and empty beer bottles and used…oh, never mind.

It's either an abandoned or never-used railway tunnel that may have been built by the Grand Trunk Railway. The legend goes that if you light a match or lighter (any small flame will do) while you're standing in the centre of the tunnel, you'll hear a bone-chilling scream and your flame will blow out! Some variations on this legend say you have to light the match at midnight.

The explanation for the screaming and blowing out is something to do with an abused girl (now a ghost) who's afraid of fire. That's why she screams and blows out the flames.

Some stories claim the girl was set on fire by her father in a divorce dispute. Others claim she was raped in the tunnel (though that one doesn't link to the flame thing very well). Still others say she ran screaming and alight from a nearby burning farmhouse and died in the tunnel. The stories are as varied and creepy as you can imagine, matching this dark and stinky tunnel toe to toe for its creep factor.

~ Big, Gargantuan & Ridiculously Oversized ~

The "World's Largest Turtle" is located in Turtleford, Saskatchewan...
and in Boissevain, Manitoba. Say what? That's right, both towns
have a giant turtle statue that, measured from beak to tail, is 8.5
metres long...or tall. Besides variations in colour, the two turtles
are pretty much alike, except in Turtleford, "Ernie" is posed on all
fours, whereas in Boissevain, "Tommy" stands tall and proud on his
back legs. Tommy also holds Canadian and American flags in his
front hands/feet/turtlegrapplers? I guess the good people of
Turtleford were looking for realism with their giant turtle (turtles
have flippers and not hands, so can't really hold flags). And
Boissevain? I guess they were looking to bring together the people of two great turtle-loving nations.

Gruesome
and Ghoulish

Some of the weirdest places in this country have to do with the macabre, the gruesome and the ghoulish. If you are really up for some weird treats, you can tour the home of a murdered Irish family in Biddulph, Ontario, or you can make a jaunt to Kootenay Lake in BC to see the house built of embalming fluid bottles. No stink. No kidding?

But not to be outdone, there are a great many scary ghosts residing in this country in some very public spaces. You'll want to sneak up on them before they sneak up on you, or else you'll be the subject of a fright and suffer a big "boo" and maybe be pushed over the edge and find yourself crying "boo-hoo-hoo." Our motto here: "Scare the ghosts before they scare you." Read on, if you dare...

THE GRUESOME

THE DONNELLY HOMESTEAD
BIDDULPH TOWNSHIP, ONTARIO

Some people might call it the enterprising idea of a smart entrepreneur who saw a need and filled it. Others would call it macabre, gruesome, ghoulish, sick, scary and in bad taste. Either way, the publicity is likely welcome, and the business thrives.

We're talking about a business that highlights, celebrates and even exploits the massacre of five members of an Irish immigrant family. Now, if it was a recent massacre, I'm sure the ghoulish factor involved in all of it would be much more in question. However, because it happened in 1880, I guess the time factor allows the macabre exploitation to seem, well… less exploitative. And to be fair, Robert Salts, who owns the Donnelly Homestead and runs the tour, is not the first person to latch onto the Donnelly story and turn it into some form of economic gain.

Let's start at the beginning. In the early morning hours of February 4, 1880, five members of an Irish immigrant family are murdered in the mad melee of a blood-soaked massacre. Killed in the melee are patriarch James Donnelly, his wife Johannah, sons Tom and John and niece Bridget. Their house is burned to the ground in the massacre. The known murderers are neighbours and town rivals of the Donnellys. There's an eyewitness to the massacre, but no one is ever convicted. And so the myth surrounding the events grows and grows until there's a bit of a book industry surrounding it and a whole niche market involving more than just a few people.

And now there's a 90-minute tour of the former homestead of the murdered family. The tour apparently includes a look at artifacts and photographs and includes a tour of the Donnelly barn. Of course, the original barn burned down, and the one in the tour was built after the murders, but that doesn't stop it from being a tour highlight—no matter how irrelevant. You see, Salts thinks the barn is haunted.

I wonder if the tour contains moments like: "We think this is where Tom was pitch forked," or "This is thought to be where Johannah Donnelly swore vengeance on the murderers and took a last puff of her pipe."

Ghostly happenings surrounding the homestead have also been reported, including the murdered family materializing, horses being spooked and horses dying as a result of travelling the Roman Line (so named for the numerous Roman Catholic families who lived there) on the anniversary of the massacre. Talk about being tough on the animals!

The Donnelly Homestead site is located in Biddulph Township near Lucan—that's halfway between London and Exeter, Ontario.

~ Big, Gargantuan & Ridiculously Oversized ~

Well, it's not so weird finding totem poles in British Columbia, but they have got some unique ones. In fact, the province has cornered the market on big totems, and they'll soon be trading on the Vancouver Stock Exchange…kidding. The "World's Largest in Diameter Totem Pole" was carved by renowned West Coast artist Richard Hunt for the city of Duncan in 1988. The totem is 7.3 metres high and is 2.1 metres in diameter at its top. Duncan is also known as the "City of Totems." Before Duncan got its wide-body totem, Victoria already had the "World's Tallest Free-Standing Totem Pole." It was carved in 1956 from a single tree by a team that included Kwakwaka'wakw artist Mungo Martin. This very tall totem is located in Beacon Hill Park and stands a whopping 38.8 metres high. Victoria's tall totem title was usurped—albeit on a technicality—in 1972, when Alert Bay, BC, erected what is now known as the "World's Tallest Totem Pole." The technicality is that Alert Bay's 52.7-metre totem is made of two pieces, whereas Victoria's is just a one piece—sort of the sports model versus the bikini. The Alert Bay totem is unique in another respect. Most totems are specific to a particular family, but the 13 figures on the Alert Bay totem represent various tribes of the Kwakwaka'wakw Nation. It is located at the northern end of Cormorant Island (off the northeast coast of Vancouver Island), on the outskirts of the Nimpkish reserve.

THE GLASS HOUSE
BOSWELL, BRITISH COLUMBIA

So, just what does a retired mortician do with his newly found spare time? Well, he takes up house building, of course! But he can't remove himself from his former profession entirely, so he incorporates the former tools of his trade into a house—literally. So, what the heck am I talking about?

Well, the mortician can't use cadavers as building materials. I mean, that would be really gruesome. However, he does go on a campaign across western Canada to collect bottles from his friends in the profession. What kind of bottles? If he'd been a doctor, they'd probably be urine sample bottles. But no, David Brown collected half a million rectangular embalming fluid bottles.

In 1952, Brown began building his dream home overlooking Kootenay Lake using those same embalming fluid bottles. He used mortar to stick the bottles together to create a two-storey castle design, complete with watchtowers. The house was apparently a great success and a comfortable place to live until curious passersby started knocking on the door night and day to see the house. That's when Brown moved out of the Glass House and turned it into a tourist attraction. It remains such today.

I've been told the whole place has the stink of death surrounding it! Not really. Brown cleaned out all the bottles before reusing them. Or at least, one would assume he did…

The Glass House is located at 11341 Highway 3A, 40 kilometres north of Creston, BC.

AND NOW…
THE GHOULISH

Step into my lair and I'll tell you a tale of the evil that men do.
You'll hear about the scary, the ghouls without heads, the logs and
dogs and places where the undead spring out and say "Boo!" So,
come on in if you dare and learn where folklore and urban legend
meet and a terrifying mix of ghoulish fun begins.

DALTON HALL, UNIVERSITY OF PRINCE EDWARD ISLAND
CHARLOTTETOWN, PEI

Dalton Hall opened in 1919 and was only the second building to be constructed for Saint Dunstan's College at UPEI.
The five-level, red brick building sports a slate roof with
prominent dormers and bay windows with decorative stone
surrounds. It's a fusion of Victorian, Edwardian and Georgian
styles—pick a monarch, it's got them all! Oh, and it's creepy.
Just the type of place an urban legend could grow up around.
And it has.

The legend is folkloric and tragic and makes for a wonder-
fully gruesome story that may or may not be true! Such is
the stuff that legends are made of.

As the story goes, two roommates were out tying one on.
A blustery snowstorm blew in, and the guys started back to
their residence, Dalton Hall. For whatever reason, the two
friends were separated, and one arrived at the Hall ahead of
the other. When the second arrived, the priests (who were the
traditional gatekeepers of this residence at what was an institution originally founded for young men aspiring to the priest-
hood) had locked all the doors, intending to teach a curfew

lesson to the tardy student. He tried frantically to get inside, but to no avail.

Later that night, the first student heard a knock at his door and assumed it was his roomie. But when he answered the door, all that greeted him was a chilling draft of air that blew past him and a trail of water that led from his room to the staircase. The next morning, the second student was found outside the front door, frozen to death.

Ever since, a chilly breeze and a trail of water leading to the staircase often confront staff and students working late on blustery winter nights. Is this a reminder of the student who died an icy death? Or perhaps it's just a drafty old building with a mysterious incontinence problem.

ST. PAUL'S ANGLICAN CHURCH
HALIFAX, NOVA SCOTIA

St. Paul's is probably known to most as the oldest Protestant church in Canada. It's been serving Protestants since 1750. A pupil of Sir Christopher Wren designed the church, and its simple wooden design is essentially comprised of a box structure with a peaked roof and a steeple at one end. The building has seen a few additions over the years, including side wings and a chancel, but it's still a simple structure.

The church is located in the centre of Halifax. It's seen battles, been scarred and has survived a great many things that much of the rest of Halifax has not. It even survived the Halifax Explosion, which, as some may know, is still considered the world's largest non-nuclear explosion. In that 1917 disaster, two ships collided in the harbour, then exploded and flattened the city.

That's where the ghostly presence of one of those victims comes into play with St. Paul's. It seems ("seems" being the key word, meaning that it may or may not be true) that during the explosion a man (or clergyman) was blown clean through the glass on the Argyle Street side of the church. In the process, the man's silhouette was etched into the glass and continues to be visible. So, why not replace the creepy etching? Well, apparently it's been tried, but each time the glass is replaced, the silhouette of the exploding man appears yet again.

That's the story, though no one will confirm its veracity— which means the whole thing could really be true, or the apparition could be a shadow cast on the glass by one of the newer buildings on the block...or dirt...or nothing at all...or something strange and evil...or a marketing ploy... or...

~ Big, Gargantuan & Ridiculously Oversized ~

The "World's Largest Beaver" sits proudly on top of a log next to Highway 43 in (where else?) Beaverlodge, Alberta. The beaver is 4.6 metres high, 5.5 metres from nose to tail and 3 metres wide. The log he sits on is 6.1 metres long.

HALIBURTON HOUSE
WINDSOR, NOVA SCOTIA

Haliburton House in Windsor, Nova Scotia, is the former home of Judge Thomas Chandler Haliburton. It's a quiet little wooden manse all decked out in white with a slow-peaked roof and large windows. Built in 1836 and expanded upon after Chandler sold it in 1856 to move to England, the home overlooks Windsor and the Avon River. In terms of being creepy, well the house itself is charming and bright. But read on...

Thomas Chandler Haliburton was an immensely popular humorist who wrote the *Sam Slick* series of books. In the 1830s and 1840s, those books popularized phrases like "it's raining cats and dogs," "quick as a wink" and "facts are stranger than fiction"—which brings us to the house's scary ghost tale. Are facts indeed stranger than fiction?

The Judge was known for his humour, which might explain the fact that he left his face behind. What's that? Another face misplaced? Dump it in the lost and found!

On occasion, the Judge's smiling face can be seen coming through the wall in the reception hall of his beloved house. He may find it funny, but a disembodied face pushing through the period wallpaper is not a Benny Hill moment.

Other versions of this weird tale tell of the "Joking Judge" emerging from a secret panel in the reception hall and walking about the house. The "face" version of the story seems more the Judge's style, if you ask me. After all, no self-respecting ghost needs a secret panel to enter a room...unless he's about to be unmasked as a hoaxer by a bunch of med-dling kids and their Great Dane.

There's not much of an explanation as to why the Judge—or just his face—haunts this place. Could be that his first wife died while he owned the property or because he created Sam Slick here or just because it's a pretty place.

In any event, if you're in the Windsor area, go take a boo at the Judge's house or just see if you can catch some face time with the old joker. Come on, who doesn't respond to a smiling face?

VICTORIA GOLF CLUB
OAK BAY, BRITISH COLUMBIA

For more than a century, people have been hearing "Fore!" shouted near the Municipality of Oak Bay, BC. It's not a ghost or anything else gruesome, just middle-aged men in ill-fitting, plaid polyester pants playing golf. The Victoria Golf Club was founded here in 1893. It's the oldest golf club in Canada still on its original site, which just happens to be a rocky point overlooking the Strait of Juan de Fuca at the southern end of Vancouver Island. You can almost picture the craggy outcroppings, the fog and a dark and blustery night, can't you?

Since the 1930s, someone or something has been haunting the seventh green. Haunting the seventh green of the Victoria Golf Club in Oak Bay sounds kind of classy, doesn't it? It's probably a former lady golfer who was kept from the PGA tour—perhaps a story of sport and woe. But no.

There's not a lot to indicate that the ghost of Doris Gravlin is any sort of golf enthusiast...or that her former self was, for that matter. In fact, considering the circumstances of her death, old Doris probably has a bit of a golf tee on her shoulder.

It seems that Doris was strangled by her husband on the seventh green and buried in a sand trap. Talk about an ignominious end! But not actually an end. Doris is still there, in ghostly form that is, and she has often been seen right there on the seventh green. She's most frequently seen wearing a long, white wedding gown, but has also taken on the form of lights. Doris has been known to play chicken with passing motorists and even scare the heck out of some by entering their cars.

No word on exactly why her husband killed her, but the old girl sounds like a hoot, if you ask me! A ghoulish hoot!

FAIRMONT BANFF SPRINGS HOTEL
BANFF, ALBERTA

Located in Banff National Park, the Fairmont Banff Springs Hotel is nestled in the lush greenery of the Bow Valley among the majestic peaks of the Rockies and overlooks the Bow River. Styled after a Scottish baronial castle, the hotel is large and made from brown stone, with deeply peaked roofs and creepy-looking dormer windows.

The hotel was originally built by the CPR and only accessible by railway. It was the grandeur of the hotel that brought people to Banff, as well as the mineral spas. The original hotel opened in 1888, and the new, improved Banff Springs was rebuilt in the 1920s. And this leads to the hauntings... But first, a story.

So, I'm attending the Banff Television Festival at the Banff Springs Hotel in the spring of 2005. Scary, creepy and beyond gruesome! Anyway, this has got to be one the creepiest buildings you could ever visit. There are all these dark and gothic-like hallways. There are halls that go nowhere, rather dimly lit passages and nooks and crannies that you can stumble upon, but never find your way back to. And the whole place is rather dark.

Sitting on a bench collecting my thoughts, I'm trying to stay away from the kids who keep asking if I'm Trina McQueen or Fred Nicolaidis, and a rather odd woman approaches and sits down beside me. She doesn't say anything, but just sits there in a white wedding gown. I figured she was someone doing publicity for some "ripped from the headlines" CTV movie. That is, until she gets up, goes to the top of the stairs, turns around and starts down. The train of her gown then gets caught on a huge candelabra, and her dress catches on fire. She panics and rolls down the stairs. I figured out it wasn't a publicity stunt, so I rushed to her. But there was no her. There was no one there at all except for me. She was gone.

This is apparently the "Bride" who regularly re-enacts her Banff Springs wedding day horror for horrified onlookers. The story goes that she broke her neck in the fall, and she's been haunting the hotel ever since. This is not in the tourist brochure.

Okay, I never really saw this, but apparently if you're there at the right time, the Bride will do her show for you. There's also a ghostly bellman named Sam who'll help you with your luggage and then disappear. Which is all you really want from a ghostly bellman, isn't it?

All I got at Banff was treated badly and a crappy bag from Rogers! A Bride sighting would have been really nice—except things like that scare the heck out of me. So, treated badly was, I guess, okay after all.

~ Big, Gargantuan & Ridiculously Oversized ~

The "World's Largest Axe" is located in Nackawic, New Brunswick. It stands 15 metres tall and is made of stainless steel embedded in concrete. Nackiwac calls itself the "Forestry Capital of Canada," so what better way to symbolize the importance of the forestry industry than an axe? Well, what about a tree? Choices, choices!

PRINCESS THEATRE
EDMONTON, ALBERTA

In the Old Strathcona part of Edmonton, the Princess
Theatre has been doing business since 1914. The theatre has
hosted vaudeville shows, Hollywood movies and even some
blue ones. It's got a large marquee out front, and the inside
has been restored to its bygone glory—plush red seating, a
balcony and an arched roof that sports cherubs. There is also
a smaller theatre in the basement. With 90 years of history,
this place has seen it all...including a ghost or two.

As the story goes, a projectionist was doing his thing in the
projection booth. All of a sudden, he heard someone knocking at the projection booth window...the window that is two
storeys up, looks out onto the street and is not accessible by
anyone that is gravity-bound. When the projectionist looked
out, what he saw was someone, something, some "being"
floating two storeys up. The only explanation is a sprite with
a sense of humour and no vertigo...or wacky kids playing a
trick...or a barrage balloon that learned to knock at the
window...or...

MAHOGANY MANOR GUEST HOUSE
ST. JOHN, NEW BRUNSWICK

The Mahogany Manor Guest House is located on Germain
Street in St. John, New Brunswick. A local merchant named
William Cross built the manor in a hodgepodge of mixed
architectural styles at the turn of the 20th century. And as
we've seen with mixed architectural styles, that spells ghost-
story creepy!

Mr. Cross has long since passed on, but his good lady wife
refuses to vacate the premises. Perhaps she thinks she's one of

the fixtures that were sold with the house. She makes herself known on occasion when she materializes walking down the stairway, swinging a lantern as she descends. That's her whole shtick. Not very creative, but she'd freak the heck out of me. That's why I like to stick to the big chain hotels. More chance that the bedspread's never been laundered, but you're less likely to run into a ghost. Eeewww on both counts!

HOTEL VANCOUVER
VANCOUVER, BRITISH COLUMBIA

The present incarnation of the Hotel Vancouver is in the tradition of those grand Canadian hotels like the Château Laurier and the Royal York. Situated in downtown Vancouver, the hotel's distinctly green, copper-topped, peaked roofs dominate the skyline. The current Hotel Vancouver was completed in 1939 and built in the French Château style. It's a rather large, bunker-like structure, with ornate dormers and scary gargoyles. The opulent interior also contains some creepy spaces.

Like other grand railway hotels, there's also a bit of mystery here. Well, not that much mystery, just a whole lot of folk-lore. One of the hotel's elevators has often been known to stop on the 14th floor, even though the stop isn't requested. As the doors part and elevator patrons wonder "What gives?" a ghostly woman in red glides down the hallway...and then she's gone. It's always the Woman in Red, isn't it?

The legend, though interesting, appears to have no real explanation. But let's face it, when did truth or "real explana-tion" ever get in the way of a ghost story?

~ Big, Gargantuan & Ridiculously Oversized ~

In the town of Upsala, Ontario, northwest of Thunder Bay, there's a kitschy statue at the Can-Op service station of a giant mosquito carrying off a man. The mosquito also has a knife and fork in its hands…legs…feet…whatever those appendages are called.

Haunted Homes, Hostels and Theatres

I think every kid growing up knows of a building in the neighbourhood that is supposedly haunted. For me, growing up in Hamilton, Ontario, that building was a house that stood at the southwest corner of Manning and Hester on Hamilton's mountain. When I was a student at Ridgemount Public School, I passed that house just about every day. It was simply known to all as the "haunted house." It was two storeys high, I think—some kind of split-level place—and all the images I remember about that house involve it being devoid of colour, dark, mysterious and spooky. It had broken windows all around, and the front door was sometimes ajar and closed at other times, adding to the idea of ghosts coming and going. I'd heard stories of kids going into that house and having the wits scared out of them and even stories about kids entering but never leaving. These were talked about, but never with names or confirmation of the events. But that didn't matter—the house was evil! And as I later found out, with most ghost stories and haunted houses, confirmation is elusive. ☞

The house had become haunted, so our kid folklore said, when the youngest son in the house murdered his parents. Apparently the place still ran with blood, which of course kept drying up and making the house darker and more evil. One day, someone dared me to go into that house. I actually tried, slowly making my way across the overgrown lawn. I even put a foot on the porch. But then I heard the sounds of a creaking floorboard or a blood-curdling scream—I'm not sure which. So, I turned tail and ran. I never ever got that close to the "haunted house" again. It was then, and still remains for me today, the weirdest place in Canada.

Ghost stories have always scared the heck out of me. They still do. While writing this book, I had terrible nightmares about the ghosts and ghost stories I was writing about. And that is why today I turn to the ghost stories I like. This chapter covers the fun ghosts. Fun ghosts, you ask? That's right, and for some reason there are a great many Canadian places haunted by benign, benevolent and just plain mischievously fun ghosts. These ghosts really just want to be noticed. They aren't out to scare you or drive you away. They aren't headless, limbless or screaming. And they don't remain, wherever they live, just to claim exclusive squatters' rights. These are the ghosts that rearrange the furniture, swing a light in the window, puff a pipe, toss some popcorn your way, put the theatre ☞

seats up, sing, perhaps let their smelly presence be known or even clip-clap-clop along with their hooves on the top floor of a hotel.

These are my kinds of ghosts—those who want to have a little fun, don't want to be forgotten, and aren't out to scare.

Oh, and by the way, I was never so surprised as an adult as when I went back to Hamilton and discovered the "haunted house" was occupied...by humans. The whole place had been transformed into a brightly coloured sub-urban home where a family lived. A manicured lawn and a car in the driveway were its new assets. It was a shocker. I wanted to go up to the door and ask if they knew what evil was in that house before they moved in. But the place still scared the bejeezes out of me. Bright paint and a freshly cut lawn couldn't take the evil away. Anyway, forget that and read on about all our fun Canadian ghosts! No one's going to jump out and say "boo" in this chapter. Whew!

CASS SCIENCE HALL, UNIVERSITY OF PRINCE EDWARD ISLAND
CHARLOTTETOWN, PEI

Cass Science Hall opened in 1939 and was the original science building for St. Dunstan's College at UPEI. The four-level structure is made of concrete block and face brick. It got its current name in 1967, in memory of Father Frederick Cass, the first priest to teach chemistry at the school. His kind devotion to the campus, the building and his students created a lasting legacy that includes a ghost that just doesn't want to leave.

Apparently, a grateful Father Cass is so enthralled with the building and the fact it was renamed in his honour that he continues to hang about. But just as he was kindly, helpful and an all around boon to society in life, he continues to be that way in death.

Father Cass is a priest of the first order, continuing to help his students from beyond. He roams the halls of the building looking for any and all problems, safety concerns or untidiness. He's been known to shut off Bunsen burners, shut down the gas mains and put equipment into tidy piles. And he does all of this without ever being seen—like when my mother used to clean my room. I knew some entity had been there, but I couldn't prove it.

The good Father just looks for ways to help avoid disaster, and he does so in the most unobtrusive ways possible. He's not a scary priest, nor a hairy beast—he's just a top-notch ghostly guy with a penchant for safety. And no pension, I guess.

FAIRMONT HOTEL MACDONALD
EDMONTON, ALBERTA

This grand old lady of Edmonton has been host to politicians and pop stars, the restless and the royal, the living and the dead. No, really! Built in the Château style in 1915, the hotel Macdonald was named for Canada's first prime minister. Like many of the great railway hotels, it is copper topped and faced with Indiana limestone. The oh, so *trés* elegant hotel overlooks the North Saskatchewan River, and views from the newer turret suites in the former attic are quite spectacular. Being in a former attic, the rooms are probably also a little creepy. Solid, Victorian and a little creepy is what all of these grand, old palaces have in common. The "Mac" has seen some grand times and fallen on heaps of hard ones as well. It was nearly demolished in the 1980s, but it has found its way back, ghosts and all.

Well, the official word is that there are no ghosts. But as the folklore goes, during the hotel's construction in 1915, a bunch of horses worked and died in the basement. And now patrons and employees alike claim on a regular basis to hear the clip-clopping of hooves on the basement's concrete floor. Officially, no one's heard a darn thing.

Worse than the pitter-patter of hooves in the basement are the sounds of a horse and carriage racing the halls of the hotel's top floor. Talk about your show ponies!

~ Big, Gargantuan & Ridiculously Oversized ~

The "World's Largest Lobster" can be found in Shediac, New Brunswick. He's not a real lobster, thank goodness—I mean, he is 10.7 metres long and 4.6 metres tall. He's also quite climbable. *C'est un grand homard!*

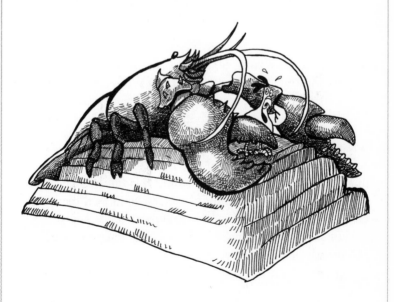

EMPRESS THEATRE
FORT MACLEOD, ALBERTA

Fort Macleod's 1912 theatre, the Empress, is the oldest operating theatre in Alberta. Originally built by the Famous Players chain, the Empress has been a vaudeville theatre, lecture hall and movie house. Sandwiched between other buildings along Fort Macleod's historic Main Street, the distinctive red brick and elegant marquee can't help but stand out.

Inside, the theatre seats 372 people in plush red seats, including a little more than 100 in the balcony. Over the years, performers have left their mark on the theatre by autographing the walls of the basement dressing rooms. You can see the scribbles of Texas Tony and his Wonder Horse Bay Doll, the CPR Minstrels and Sammy Davis Sr. The theatre continues the tradition of using small Tiffany-style lamps for lighting, which gives the place an elegant glow and no doubt contributes to the legend that the place is haunted.

Yes, the ghost of the Empress Theatre is another unique sprite in Alberta's back pocket. "Ed" is apparently the former resident janitor, and he's either not too thrilled to be dead, not too thrilled with the place's state of cleanliness or perhaps just a bit of a curmudgeon whether dead or alive.

Ed's got a couple of issues. First off, he apparently has a rank aroma. Booze, cigarettes and cow dung are the three odours most often associated with him. But the odours may also be because Ed hangs out around the garbage. In fact, he rearranges the garbage—he's been known to flip popcorn containers out of the trash. Perhaps he's making a statement about garbage versus recyclables, but it's unlikely.

Ed also has a thing for flipping down already folded theatre seats, as if he's saying "So, is anyone sitting here? No...well, don't! Boo off!"

MACKENZIE HOUSE
TORONTO, ONTARIO

So, does the rabble-rousing newspaper editor, leader of the rebellions of 1837 and former first mayor of Toronto haunt this downtown Toronto house? Well, could be. There are, in fact, some people who think Mackenzie House is the most haunted place in Toronto. There are also people who think that the statue of Winston Churchill at Nathan Phillips Square talks. I certainly don't think the latter is true.

The house is situated in the heart of downtown Toronto. It's a gas-lit Greek revival, Victorian row house. Funny, how when you attach "Victorian" to something, it conjures up creepy nighttime images including fog, huh? Friends of W.L. Mackenzie took up a collection for him when he retired and bought the house. It changed hands several times after his death and was once even a boarding house. It's nearly been demolished a couple of times, but before the wreckers could start, something always saved it. Coincidence or ghostly happening? You be the judge.

The house has a fully functional 19th-century print shop like the one Mackenzie used to publish his rabble-rousing newspaper. It also apparently has a rabble-rousing ghost.

That's right! People claim to have seen the apparition of a short, bald man wearing a wig and a coat. Sounds like old William Lyon Mackenzie. Apparently old W.L.M. has a thing for indoor plumbing. It wasn't there when he was an official live resident, but in his ghostly form, he likes to run the taps and set the toilet a-flushing. He was a rebel, remember— ahead of his time and an agent for change. So the restroom fascination seems completely in line.

There are a couple of other ghosts hanging out in the house as well—one may be the last Mrs. Mackenzie. If you want a firsthand glimpse, head down to 82 Bond Street in Toronto and just ask the staff about the ghosts and the exorcism. They're quite happy to tell you about all of it. It's all an 1837-like rebellious hoot!

LAST CHANCE SALOON, ROSEDEER HOTEL
WAYNE, ALBERTA

Ten miles and 11 bridges south of Drumheller, Alberta, you'll come to the genuine, certified ghost town of Wayne. And within that former coal boomtown of the 1920s and 1930s, you'll come to the historic landmark, the Rosedeer Hotel. The hotel is a three-storey wooden slab of a structure that has changed little since 1913, except that over the years, a ghost has taken up residence inside its Last Chance Saloon.

Well, there's not a lot to say about the ghost at the Last Chance Saloon. He's thought to be the former owner. Seems to be taking a load off and sittin' a spell. His only eerie activity? He puffs a nice little pipe. And the aroma is cheery, not eerie. So head on over to Wayne and see if he'll offer you a puff. If he does, I'm sure you'll be quite chuffed… Take your camera.

CANMORE OPERA HOUSE, CALGARY HERITAGE PARK
CALGARY, ALBERTA

The Canmore Opera House is a log cabin located in Calgary's Heritage Park. The structure was actually used by Alberta Theatre Projects (ATP) for its first 13 years of operation.

Even though ATP has moved on, its productions must have inspired at least one of the Opera House's permanent residents. Apparently, on occasion, the voice of a beautiful songstress can be heard. She's wily and shy, though, because she never materializes in human form. But it's that voice that visitors swear they'll never forget.

~ Big, Gargantuan & Ridiculously Oversized ~

The "World's Largest Badminton Racket" can be found just north of Edmonton in the town of St. Albert, Alberta. In fact, you can't miss it—it's 4.3 metres tall, though it's skinny, like badminton rackets will be, so if you blink, I can't guarantee you'll see it. It stands tall and proud outside the Red Willow Badminton Club on Boudreau Road.

MASONIC TEMPLE
WINNIPEG, MANITOBA

Winnipeg's former Masonic Temple has housed many businesses over the years, including a Mother Tucker's restaurant. It is located at the intersection of Donald Street and Ellice Avenue in the 'Peg. It's a heavy, imposing structure (as Masonic Temples generally are) that dates back to 1895.

People have been talking about the building's mischievous sprite for years. He/she/it even once made an appearance in a CBC news report. Starring with Knowlton Nash didn't go to the sprite's head, because it continued its antics.

The lights have been known to flicker, and former restaurant workers claim on more than occasion to have come to work in the morning and discovered that some mystery rearrangements had taken place. Some suggested the ghost partied all night long, spending precious sprite time moving salt and pepper shakers and using all the napkins.

The ghost has also been known to do a bit of toe tapping in the attic. One former employee even said he'd seen the ghost decked out in 18th-century costume. The haunting is, of course, attributed to some evil done by the Masons in times gone by.

But who cares, really? Just go try the napkins…the ghost swears by them!

~ Big, Gargantuan & Ridiculously Oversized ~

At the junction of Highways 97 and 16 in British Columbia stands an 8.2-metre-tall mascot named Mr. PG. That's right, Mr. PG—"P" and "G" being the initials representing the community's name, Prince George. Mr. PG has a replica wooden log as a body, sports a yellow hard hat and waves a flag. The original Mr. PG was actually made of logs, but unfortunately, he eventually rotted away. The new, improved Mr. PG is made of metal painted to look like wood. Prince George is, of course, a logging community and the "Northern Capital of British Columbia." On special occasions, Mr. PG gets dressed up. He wears a tutu during the city's dance festival and sports a white cane and dark glasses for CNIB Week. It sounds like Mr. PG is quite the gad-about-town!

Nature's So Nutty

Reversing falls, magnetic hills, white squirrels, black squirrels, sand dunes, pink lakes that are green, water, water everywhere, Hell's Gate and pingos. Take your pick. Whichever you choose, the naturally nutty nature of nature is, well…unnatural, naturally speaking.

Does that make any sense? Not really, but nothing outdoes the nutty nature of nature. It confounds, discombobulates and defies explanation—except by scientists, psychics and parapsychologists—provides tourist attractions and gives a bit of mystery to some places that might otherwise seem ordinary. Nature is so weird!

THE REVERSING FALLS
ST. JOHN, NEW BRUNSWICK

Although a bit of a misnomer, the "Reversing Falls" are indeed a phenomenon that happens nowhere else in the world… And no, it's not an optical illusion or something faked to get tourists to come see.

Some of the highest tides in the world are those of the Bay of Fundy. And twice a day, those enormous Bay of Fundy tides crash into the St. John River, forcing the river to flow backwards—in reverse, you might say!

Here are the details. Tidewater flows through the mouth of St. John Harbour and meets the downward-flowing St. John River. This is where the so-called "Reversing Falls" are created. The opposing flows of tidewater and the St. John River meet and create violent rapids as the water smashes into river-bottom ridges and is then forced through a bottleneck gorge.

The whole thing happens in reverse at high tide. (Ah, so that's where the moniker "Reversing Falls" comes from.) The falls, however, are not so much falls as they are turbulent rapids.

At high tide, the water in the harbour rises, then stops and pushes the St. John River backwards. Talk about nature's fury. The reverse flow is felt as far as 130 kilometres upstream at Fredericton.

Interestingly, the whole magical tidal action starts in the southern Indian Ocean, makes a right turn around the Cape of Good Hope and then makes a beeline for the Bay of Fundy. With that kind of run up, the St. John River doesn't stand a chance. That is some kick!

SKOOKUMCHUK RAPIDS
BRITISH COLUMBIA

Skookumchuk…Skookumchuk…Skookumchuk… That's just fun to say, isn't it? Skookumchuck is a word that comes from the Chinook language and means "turbulent water," which the "Skook" definitely is. The rapids actually appear to be boiling, as huge volumes of water are forced through the Skookumchuck Narrows.

In some ways, it's similar to the reversing falls in St. John, NB, since at the change of the tides, the flow of salt water switches and reverses the direction and power of the rapids. On a 3-metre tide, as much as 909 billion litres of water are squeezed through the narrows that connect Sechelt and Jervis Inlets. The most dramatic and visible motions occur when those billions of litres of water are sucked through cavernous whirlpools, creating standing waves.

The dramatic sight is easiest seen and experienced one hour after slack tide. Slack tide is, of course, when the narrows become flat and calm at either peak high tide or peak low tide. Of course! The whole thing can be rather dangerous, though the rapids attract surfers and kayakers from all over the world who want to experience the 10–14-knot currents. The effect is almost like a natural version of a wave pool at one of those water parks we all flock to in the summer.

The Skookumchuk Rapids are located in Skookumchuck Narrows Provincial Park, at the north end of the Sechelt Peninsula on the beautiful Sunshine Coast of British Columbia.

~ Big, Gargantuan & Ridiculously Oversized ~

It's an all-Prairie final in the "World's Largest Bee" category. And the winner is…Fahler, Alberta, with a bee measuring nearly 7 metres long. The "Honey Bee" in Tisdale, Saskatchewan, is only 5 metres long. Hang in there, Tisdale, you've got more weird things to offer!

HELL'S GATE
BRITISH COLUMBIA

The mighty water of the Fraser River being squeezed through a narrow gorge definitely creates a dramatic and turbulent sight to see. At Hell's Gate in the BC Interior, as much as 757 million litres of water are squeezed through a narrow 35-metre-wide gorge. All that water happens at spring runoff, and Hell's Gaters are quite proud to point out that it's twice the volume of water flowing over Niagara Falls.

This mighty whitewater area was named by Simon Fraser, who scaled the canyon's walls. There's an "air-tram," which is basically a cable car that travels over the river, giving visitors a great view. People have also been known to walk the suspension bridge just to freak themselves out.

It's a dangerous place, but there is a great story about a blind cow that found herself in the river and somehow managed to survive the violence of Hell's Gate. She was dubbed "Rosebank Rosie," and though cows don't swim, they apparently float pretty well. I'll bet it's their big, buoyant udders!

~ Big, Gargantuan & Ridiculously Oversized ~

Located on the western shore of Lake Winnipeg, Gimli, Manitoba, calls itself the "Capital of New Iceland" as a trubute to the Icelandic origins of many of its early immigrants. In ancient Norse mythology, Gimli was also known as the home of the gods. So what better centennial project to build than a 4.6-metre-tall fibreglass Viking? The Gimli Chamber of Commerce did just that way back in 1967. The structure was designed by a professor from the University of Manitoba and sculpted, horns and all, by the late George Barone. The Viking was unveiled in a grand ceremony in July 1967 by the then-president of Iceland, Ásgeir Ásgeirsson.

THE POCKET DESERT
OSOYOOS, BRITISH COLUMBIA

Dubbed the only "true" desert in Canada (because, I guess, the rest of the pretenders are lying), the Pocket Desert is located at the southernmost tip of the Okanagan Valley. It's also one of the most fragile and endangered ecosystems in North America and contains one of Canada's largest concentrations of at-risk species—more than 100 rare plants and more than 300 rare invertebrates. Some of those species include: the tiger salamander, sage thrasher, night snake and badger.

At the Osoyoos Desert Centre, visitors can walk along a boardwalk through a protected portion of the habitat. At the Desert Centre, the staff educates, does research and even validates parking—the first two, anyhow.

TUKTUYAKTUK PENINSULA
NORTHWEST TERRITORIES

The world's largest concentration of pingos is located on the Tuktuyaktuk Peninsula in the Northwest Territories. There may, in fact, be as many as 1450 pingos on the peninsula. So, just what the heck are pingos? Officially, it's an Inuit word meaning "conical hill." Which doesn't really clarify much, does it?

Pingos actually look like small volcanoes and range from 15 metres to almost half a kilometre across. They are, in fact, conical hills that often have a crater lake in the centre. Pingos have also been described as nothing more than nature's pimples. Their formation involves permafrost and standing water—all too complicated and uninteresting to read about, especially as compared to nature's magic!

Oh, and pingos aren't to be confused with that cartoon show about the penguin named Pingu. They are totally different. However, Pingu getting lost down a pingo sounds good to me! That little penguin drives me crazy.

GREAT SAND HILLS
LIEBENTHAL, SASKATCHEWAN

Sand dunes are not something you probably think of when you think about southwestern Saskatchewan. I mean, if you happen to think of southwestern Saskatchewan at all. But from now on, when you do think of southwestern Saskatchewan, think "Sand Hills!" In fact, think "Great Sand Hills"!

Twenty kilometres northeast of Liebenthal, Saskatchewan, you'll run into 1900 km^2 of active dunes, high, stable dunes and sand flats. These sand hills are what remain of a delta from an ancient glacier. Yet another thing I wouldn't have thought about when thinking about southwestern Saskatchewan.

The stable dunes make up most of what are the Great Sand Hills. They are covered with sagebrush, prairie grasses and other plants. The active dunes make up only a small part of the area (about 1%), but they also provide a crazy view. The place looks more like a little corner of the Sahara than it does like Saskatchewan. The active dunes change size and shape over time and are known to grow to 12 metres or more in height.

If you visit, sandals or desert boots are definitely the designated footwear of the day!

MAGNETIC HILL
MONCTON, NEW BRUNSWICK

For more than 70 years, savvy boosters from the New Brunswick berg of Moncton have been pushing their odd little tourist attraction known as Magnetic Hill. There are other magnetic hills, but none top the one near Moncton. They'll tell you: drive to the bottom of the hill, take your foot off the brake and put your car in neutral. You'll be absolutely amazed as your car coasts uphill! It works with trucks and vans and buses as well. Or so it would seem.

Here's a little secret about Magnetic Hill. There is absolutely nothing magnetic about it. Except, that is, for its ability to draw tourists. In fact, the whole thing is an optical illusion in which a slight downhill grade looks like an uphill grade. What looks like the bottom of the hill is actually the top of the hill. It's your eyes playing tricks on you, not the geography (in addition to a little sleight-of-hand marketing that's been done by some wily New Brunswickers).

There are many places around the world where a similar optical illusion can be experienced. It usually occurs on stretches of road where the level horizon is obscured and visual clues such as trees growing at an angle, not truly vertical.

This tedious, yet accurate description hasn't stopped the Moncton's Magnetic Mafia. They've been talking about Magnetic Hill since the 1800s, when, before there were cars, wagons rolled backwards up the hill…and I'll bet before that, Ezekiel's wheel rolled up the hill as well.

If you're looking to visit this most famous of Canada's growing number of magnetic hills, take exit 450 from the Trans-Canada Highway (#2) and follow the signs. Hopefully, they're right side up and not being dragged uphill by the perpetual motion of Moncton marketing gurus.

CÔTE MAGNÉTIQUE
CHARTIERVILLE, QUÉBEC

Not nearly as famous as Moncton's Magnetic Hill, nor as touristy nor as commercially marketed, the Côte Magnétique (Magnetic Hill) just outside Chartierville, Québec, is nonetheless just another optical illusion. And unlike the marketing minions of Moncton, here at Chartierville they admit the whole thing is quite natural. Although, that is perhaps why it's not as famous as the one at Moncton. I mean, a little magic, mystery and wonder goes a long way in drawing a crowd.

Chartierville is about 8 kilometres from the New Hampshire border. The instructions for experiencing this little bit of eye trickery are prominently displayed on a sign beside the road in both French and English. Those instructions read as follows: "Stop here. Put car in neutral. Look behind and experiment. Have a nice day!" Or, in French: *Arrêtez ici. Mettez le véhicule au point mort (N). Regardez en arrière et expérimentez. Bonne journée!* Bilingual, fun and polite! *Bonne route!*

MAGNETIC HILL
BURLINGTON, ONTARIO

Is it evil, I ask ya? Eeevvvilll? Ah…no!

The magnetic hill in Burlington, Ontario, is starting to rival the one in Moncton for fame. And that is mainly because a cheesy television show perpetuated mysterious folkloric tales involving the hill, many car accidents and the ghosts of children who died in a bus crash.

However, Burlington's Magnetic Hill is no more a mystery, magnetic or ghostly than any of the others. It is an optical illusion, pure and simple. I grew up in Hamilton, a stone's throw from Burlington's Magnetic Hill. I've been there many times and never felt anything creepy, dead-kid related or ghostly about it. And, as far as I can tell, there is no record of the purported bus crash. However, facts have never kept TV shows like *Creepy Canada* nor TV channels like CTV Travel from popularizing and publicizing the myth.

It has also been suggested that UFOs are somehow related to the phenomenon. Because, of course, aliens would take great pleasure in taking a jaunt over to Burlington and messing with the inhabitants' minds in the form of pulling their rather primitive vehicles backwards up a hill! I wonder what message they're trying to send to us? Perhaps it's "Boo!" or "You are such naïve fools!"

If you want to visit the Burlington Magnetic Hill, it's north of Highway 403 on a rural part of King Road. You'll want to stop your car at the Hydro right-of-way entrance to begin your ride. Make your way past the UFOs lined up on the right and ghost buses of dead kids on the left.

AND THE REST OF THE MAGNETIC HILLS...

Other magnetic hills starting to make their way into the tourist-marketing juggernaut include: Dacre, Ontario (near Pembroke); Neepawa, Manitoba; and Cantons-de-l'Est, Québec. There may also be one near Abbotsford, BC.

~ Big, Gargantuan & Ridiculously Oversized ~

In St. Thomas, Ontario, there is a life-sized statue of Jumbo, P.T. Barnum's famous giant elephant. The citizens of St. Thomas erected the statue in 1985 to commemorate the 100th anniversary of Jumbo's death. Jumbo never lived in St. Thomas, nor was he born there, and he didn't even perform there. He was unfortunately killed there when he had a run-in with a locomotive.

THE WHITE SQUIRRELS
EXETER, ONTARIO

So, do white squirrels actually exist or is this some twisted marketing campaign in which the tree rats with the furry tails are spray-painted as a come-on?

Well, actually they do exist—no paint, no come-on and no pink eyes. And that is one of the most unique things about Exeter's white squirrel population. Whereas other towns in North America promote their white albino squirrels—pink eyes and all—Exeter's white squirrels aren't albino. They are regular squirrels that just happen to be white.

And in Exeter, the townsfolk and visitors celebrate these unique tree-dwelling rodents with the annual White Squirrel Festival each September. There's a parade and white squirrel events with white squirrel mascots galore. The official mascot is named "White Wonder." Wonder why?

The origin of Exeter's white squirrels is unclear, though it's been suggested the following groups had something to do with it: Gypsies, tropical visitors and even Torontonians. If you visit Exeter other than at festival time, the white squirrels can be seen all over town and especially in MacNaughton Park. Exeter is located 50 kilometres north of London, Ontario.

THE BLACK SQUIRRELS
LONDON, ONTARIO

Not to be outdone by the Exeter mighty whites, London, Ontario, boasts a population of black squirrels in Victoria Park. No festival…yet…but these black devils were actually exported to the campus of Ohio's Kent State University in the early 1960s. I'm not exactly sure what else makes these black squirrels unique, odd or weird. I get the white squirrel oddity. Unusual, right? And a white squirrel definitely stands out in a crowd. The black ones, not so much! But what do I know?

PINK LAKE
GATINEAU PARK, QUÉBEC

For decades, people have been travelling to Gatineau Park to see the famous Pink Lake only to be disappointed when they find out the lake is actually green. The lake is actually named for a family of settlers, the Pinks, who originally settled the area in the early 1800s.

But Pink Lake isn't just an absurd colour mix-up. It does, in fact, fall under the category of "Nature's So Nutty." Why? Well, Pink Lake is actually a "meromictic" lake, which means that because of its depth, small surface and sheltered positioning, its waters do not mix. That is, the water in the lake is stratified into various layers. The bottom layer, for example, is deprived of oxygen, which means that organic matter accumulates there but does not decompose.

Not to be outdone by colour and water stratification, the lake is also home to some unique species, including the stickleback. Sticklebacks are an ancient type of fish with three spines and date back to the time when an arm of the Atlantic Ocean, called the Champlain Sea, covered the area. When the sea retreated 10,000 years ago, the stickleback got trapped. However, the crafty little devils learned to adapt to the lake environment. I guess when you have three spines, adaptation's a breeze!

MANITOULIN ISLAND
ONTARIO

So, what does being the largest freshwater lake in the world get you besides being a question on every quiz show ever broadcast on TV? Well, there are the tourists who tramp all over your beautiful wilderness and…well…the laurels. Let's not forget the laurels, because you are the "Largest Island in

a Freshwater Lake" in the whole entire world. That's 2766 km²
of island, don't ya know. Have I mentioned it's within a freshwater lake?

What is also interesting—or weird—is that there are also
110 inland lakes on Manitoulin Island. Within many of
those lakes you've also got many islands. Say what? Well
here goes: Treasure Island is within Mindemoya Lake;
Mindemoya Lake is on Manitoulin Island; Manitoulin
Island is in Georgian Bay; Georgian Bay is in Lake Huron;
Lake Huron is in North America; North America is on
Earth. That's pretty cool, eh?

Manitoulin Island…It's big and freshly watered and weird.
No, really!

ROCHE PERCÉE SANDSTONE
SASKATCHEWAN

Roche Percée is a village located in the southeastern corner of
Saskatchewan near Estevan. Just outside the village, there is
a craggy sandstone outcrop that is both oddly shaped and
"pierced." You see, Roche Percée is French for "pierced rock."

Over the centuries (maybe longer), Roche Percée has been
worn down by wind and rain and marked mainly by human
graffiti. We are such a creative species, aren't we? Names were
carved on it by members of the North-West Mounted Police
during their great trek west, Wild Bill Hickock may have left
his mark somewhere on the rock, and ancient Natives also
wrote their names on the rock with crude pictures. One of
them translates to "Kilroy was here!" Not really.

Roche Percée was once also a sacred site to local Natives.
Now, it's more or less just a weird curiosity near the
American border. Progress!

SLEEPING GIANT ISLAND
LAKE SUPERIOR, ONTARIO

Looking out across Lake Superior from Thunder Bay, you can distinctly see the form of a giant in the water with his arms folded across his muscular chest… Or that's what they say, anyway. I've kind of seen it by squinting and unfocusing my eyes as if I was looking at a Magic Eye piece of "art." The phenomenon is not (surprise, surprise) a real sleeping giant. It's the formation of flora and fauna on an island.

However, First Nations lore says the Sleeping Giant is none other than the Great Spirit, Nanabijou. The rather long and somewhat complicated legend basically says that Nanabijou awarded a loyal Ojibway tribe with access to a great silver mine, with the stipulation that they keep the location a secret from the white men or else both the Ojibway and Nanabijou would suffer the consequences. Sioux rivals coveted the silver. A seasoned Sioux scout infiltrated the Ojibway tribe, learned the mine's location and then inadvertently told it to some white men after they got him drunk. The result was as warned: Nanabijou was turned to stone and became the Sleeping Giant in the water, and the Ojibway disappeared.

It's hard to say who's to blame here—Nanabijou for his poor judgement and showing off the wealth; the Ojibway for not doing enough to protect the secret mine; the covetous Sioux who couldn't hold their liquor; or the evil white men. In the end, life's too short, grudges are pointless and Sleeping Giant Island is rather picturesque.

THE BADLANDS
ALBERTA

They've been described as an alien landscape and are characterized by erosion formations, buttes, coulees, hoodoos, winding canyons and gullies. These are Alberta's Badlands. Man, are they weird looking! And baaaad. Not street gang bad, just inhospitable, really. That's what early French settlers thought of the area. They discovered very quickly that the Badlands—*les terres mauvaises*—were not suitable for farming. Which may be one of the reasons Québec is in the east and not where Alberta is now. Location, location, location!

The heart of the Badlands is in and around the Drumheller area—about 140 kilometres north and east of Calgary. Drumheller and the Badlands are also known as "Dinosaur Country." As Canadians, we all know of the amazing dinosaur fossils discovered in the Badlands. Although the place is dry now, when dinos roamed the earth it was a thriving wetland. The Royal Tyrrell Museum is in Drumheller. It is Canada's only institution devoted entirely to paleontology. And though the museum's not exclusively about the dinosaurs, they do sit centre stage.

~ Big, Gargantuan & Ridiculously Oversized ~

A Viking ship (or at least the front half of one) greets visitors at the west end of Main Street in Erickson, Manitoba. Erickson was settled in the 1800s by Scandinavian immigrants and is known as the "Land of the Vikings." The ship is replete with red-and-white sails and two boatmen made of fibreglass. The boatmen were originally carved from wood like the boat, but were removed and later replaced after they were desecrated (their body parts were cut off and reattached in a sexually suggestive arrangement). No word on why the back half of the Viking ship was never built. Perhaps the idea wouldn't float with the town.

It's a Ghost What?
A Phantom Who?

The great outdoors seems to be a perfectly fine place to haunt, especially if all the homes, theatres, government buildings, trailers and outhouses are already taken.

The ghosts who favour the outdoors have a real creative spirit about them, too. Some disguise themselves as the sound of the whispering wind; others take a midnight ride on a horse, on the rails or on a fogbound ship.

There really are not a lot of restrictions to creeping out the great outdoors, so let's have at it…

PLACES WHERE THE GHOSTS TEND TO FLOAT

Aye's da bye dat builds da boat,
And aye's da bye dat sails her,
And aye's da ghost dat haunts near the shore,
And scares da bejeezes outta Liza.

MAHONE BAY
NOVA SCOTIA

Mahone Bay is a beautiful inlet of the Atlantic Ocean on the southeast coast of Nova Scotia. Fabled communities such as Lunenburg, Mahone Bay and Oak Island are located here. The bay is one of those almost mystical maritime places that casts a long shadow over quaint, mostly rural communities. The people are friendly, and the climate is mild year round. Although, because it's on the Atlantic Coast, Mahone Bay does not completely escape the battering winds and waves of the Atlantic Ocean. And sometimes, the fog rolls in like it's old London town. There are also more than 100 islands in the bay and just as many ghost stories.

Legend has it that on foggy nights, around the time of a full moon, the ghostly spectre of a fire ship has been observed there. The ghostly phenomenon is known as the Teaser Light and gets its name from an American privateer, the *Young Teazer*, that was chased into Mahone Bay in 1813 by a British warship. Trapped, with no way of escaping, *Young Teazer*'s crew set her ablaze to keep her from being captured.

The ship was carrying a substantial amount of ammunition. (It was the War of 1812, after all, and a ship without ammunition was like a peanut butter cup without its peanut butter— hollow and pointless!) Anyway, *Young Teazer* exploded in a spectacular fireball, and the shockwave was felt all along the shores of Mahone Bay and probably for kilometres inland. The entire crew of the ship perished in the explosion, which may explain why the ghostly ship reappears time and again. The crew is confused, I guess?

Today, landlubbers peering out into the bay are the most common spectators of the Teazer Light spectre. The ship appears through the fog, sails for a time on the bay and then disappears in a spectacular flameout. Sailors in the bay have also come a-runnin' and a-claimin' that the fiery spook ship tried to run them down. Which seems a bit far-fetched, since it's hard to come a-runnin' on water, unless you're "you know who," and he was really only ever seen walking.

As a way of commemorating the whole gruesome original death-inducing spectacle, as well as the recurring ghost ship sightings, the Mahone Bay Wooden Boat Festival sets ablaze a small replica of the *Teazer* each year.

~ Big, Gargantuan & Ridiculously Oversized ~

The "World's Largest Muskoka Chair" (or Adirondack chair, if you prefer that name) is located in Varney, Ontario. This largest wooden cottage chair is 6.7 metres high. There was some controversy over who had the biggest Muskoka chair, because the town of Gravenhurst, Ontario, also claimed the title. But at just under 4 metres high, clearly Gravenhurst's chair has come up short.

NORTHUMBERLAND STRAIT
PRINCE EDWARD ISLAND AND NOVA SCOTIA

Northumberland Strait is an arm of the Gulf of St. Lawrence
that separates Prince Edward Island from Nova Scotia and
New Brunswick. The strait is 290 kilometres long and
between 19 and 48 kilometres wide. It's big enough to get
lost in, but not so big as to be inaccessible…except in the
winter months, when it freezes over. The strait doesn't get as
cold or as wild and woolly storms as other maritime locales,
but it has its own mystery.

On cold, warm, dark, foggy, clear and windy nights, a fiery
phantom ship has often been seen on the Northumberland
Strait. Since 1876, people have been reporting sightings of
this glowing or fiery three-masted ship in the channel
between the north coast of Nova Scotia and the south coast
of PEI. But in sharp contrast to Mahone Bay's Teazer Light,
the strait's phantom ship doesn't just appear in foggy weather.
The only common weather phenomenon related to sightings
of the phantom ship seems to be that it often appears with
the advance of a northeast wind and storm. So, it's kind of
like a spectral version of that Channel 7 Accuweather warning: "There's a blowhard of a nor'easter a-comin'!"

The phantom ship sometimes starts out as a fireball and
magically transforms into a glowing ship. There are reports
of people being seen on the fire ship's deck, as well as unsuc-
cessful attempts to rescue the fiery sailors by "real" ships.
Theories as to why the phantom fire ship keeps appearing
have included pacts with the devil, pirates and a little bit of
Disney Imagineering. My theory—young kids and olde-tyme
shenanigans!

BAIE DE CHALEURS
NEW BRUNSWICK

Baie de Chaleurs is an arm of the Gulf of St. Lawrence. It separates Québec's Gaspé Peninsula from New Brunswick's north shore and extends 137 kilometres from one end to the other. That's a pretty big area. In fact, it's the largest bay in the Gulf of St. Lawrence. The name Baie de Chaleurs translates to English as "bay of warmth." However, that's just another one of those geographic jokes, since the water in the Baie can stay cold even in summer. Sandy beaches can be found all over the Baie, as well as a huge natural sandbar.

This body of water, like many others on the East Coast, is associated with remarkable tales of sightings of a fire ship. The fire ship in the Baie is not much different from that seen in Northumberland Strait. It has the requisite glowing presence, the three masts, the year-round appearances and a penchant for foretelling a storm. For 200 years, people have been reporting sightings of what the Acadians called *le feu du mauvais temps*, which of course means "bad weather fire."

There are various theories explaining this ship's appearance. They range from the ghostly reappearance of various shipwrecks to ships destroyed in battle to devilish death warnings for people on shore! More scientific reasons include rotting vegetation, natural gas being released under the ocean and St. Elmo's Fire. Translation: digestion, sea fart or a bad 1980s "Brat Pack" movie. No matter how you slice it, it's pretty silly!

THE GRAVEYARD OF THE PACIFIC
BRITISH COLUMBIA

The West Coast of Vancouver Island is known as the "Graveyard of the Pacific." More than 200 ships have foundered there since the early 19th century. Rocky shores, powerful ocean currents and stormy weather have all contributed to its well-earned moniker. Wind and rain and fog, oh my!

One of the most famous wrecks and ongoing mysteries of the "graveyard" is that of the passenger ship *Valencia*. The ship left San Francisco for Seattle in January 1906, but crashed on the rocks off Vancouver Island near Panchena Point. Attempts at evacuation and rescue were more than muddled and went on for two days. Other ships tried to help in the

IT'S A GHOST WHAT? A PHANTOM WHO?

rescue, but the *Valencia* broke apart and took at least 117 souls with her to the bottom.

Since then, a phantom ship resembling the *Valencia* has been seen steaming the Pacific near the wreck sight. Sailors have even reported seeing ghostly forms clinging to the ghost ship. Of course! What other kind of form would cling to a ghost ship? One of the most interesting aspects of the whole story is that one of the *Valencia*'s lifeboats washed up on shore in perfect shape—27 years after the ship sank. And the East Coast thought they had great ghost ship stories!

~ Big, Gargantuan & Ridiculously Oversized ~

Travelling east along Highway 14 from Saskatoon, motorists are greeted by a unique sign at the entrance to the town of Biggar, Saskatchewan. The colourful sign reads: "New York is Big, but this is Biggar." The slogan originated in 1909, courtesy of a survey crew who had too much to drink one night and decided to play a joke on the town. However, the joke was on them. The town loved the slogan and has been promoting it ever since. Oh, and by the way, the town is named after the former general counsel for the Grand Trunk Pacific Railroad, W.H. Biggar. It's not just a spelling mistake.

PLACES WHERE THE GHOSTS RIDE

SCUGOG ISLAND
ONTARIO

An hour's drive northeast of Toronto, near Port Perry, lies Scugog Island in Lake Scugog. Lake Scugog and the island were created when a dam was built at Purdy's Mills (now called Lindsay) in 1827. The lake covers 100 km², and the island is mostly rural, though it's large enough to have farms and villages. With that rural area comes the story of a lonely and desolate road island where a legend of woe has grown up.

In fact, the road is where a motorcyclist is supposed to have died and whose phantom continues to ride and haunt with vim, vigour and speed. Oh, and not much skill, since the accident that killed him in the first place in the 1950s or 1960s keeps stopping him in his tracks.

The legend says that the young man in question was trying out a motorcycle on a straight road, misjudged his speed, lost control, flew off the bike and hit his head on a rock. Oh, and he died. Judging from the type of crash, his riding skills were questionable. In any event, he apparently won't leave and making fun of him is probably not going to help.

This modern "haunting" phenomenon takes the form of a round, white light (which looks like a motorcycle headlight) that travels down the road and becomes a small red light when it passes you. So, headlight one way, brake light in the other direction. Got it? Some people have even suggested that they've heard the sounds of a motorcycle with the lights. They later had their hearing checked, but nothing was found. So they had their heads examined—still nothing!

Psychics, paranormal researchers and even reporters have examined the phenomenon. Explanations range from the reflection of car headlights, lights caused by a nearby geo-logical fault and a complete and utter hoax. Still, people who have been there swear there is something to the ghostly lights of the poor and unskilled ghostly motorcycle-riding kid! Vroom, vroom!

~ Big, Gargantuan & Ridiculously Oversized ~

The "World's Largest Oil Can" sits on the edge of town in Rocanville, Saskatchewan. It was built in 1973 to commemorate the Symons Oil Can Factory and its 50 years of continuous oper-ation. The oil can stands 7 metres tall and is bright red, so if you're driving by, there's no way you can miss it. It doesn't really contain oil, though.

ROUTE 230 BETWEEN PORT REXTON AND PORT UNION
NEWFOUNDLAND

Something freaky this way comes on the Bonavista! Route 230 between Port Rexton and Port Union, Newfoundland, is a quiet place. It's a lonely stretch of road where nary a person, nor other cars, nor beasts are encountered. So why does a phantom train or phantom hitchhiker or a combination thereof keep popping up? Who knows, but that is apparently what happens. Along this spooky route, people have reported encountering moving lights and even a phantom train running beside the road. There's no track, but there are spectres of people travelling on a ghostly train.

Also along this route, startled travellers have reported people picking up hitchhikers, only to have them disappear from the backseats of their cars when they get to their destinations. The one question I have to ask about this scenario is: If I picked up a hitchhiker, why would I let this stranger sit behind me in the backseat of my car? I mean, I'm just asking to be mugged, murdered or carjacked, aren't I? Or perhaps the drivers of these cars didn't realize it, but they are actually taxi drivers and the passengers who disappear have done a runner. You know—the old "drive and dash." Could there be an alcoholic beverage involved in these incidents? Maybe there's a little freaky "screech" action going on?

WATERFRONT SEA BUS
AND SKY TRAIN STATION
VANCOUVER, BRITISH COLUMBIA

The Waterfront Sky Train Station and Sea Bus Terminal on Cordova Street between Granville and Seymour is a rather lonely and remote part of downtown Vancouver. This is the sight of the old CPR terminal, and in fact, the station can be entered through the old railway station on Cordova Street.

This is also the place said to be haunted by the "Headless Brakeman." The questions raised by this moniker are many and varied. If he's headless, does he bump into things? If he's headless, how does he know when to brake (no eyes, no ears)? And my mother would have my head if I didn't ask this one— is he headless because he forgot his head because it wasn't attached? The answers to those questions are no, no and no.

Way back in 1928, a railway brakeman slipped off one train and was run over by another. Now, that's some bad luck! Worse, his head was severed in the accident, giving him his illustrative name. Since then he's been seen, especially on stormy nights, hopping on and off railcars (and now the Sky Train, I guess), apparently feeling around for his head. He feels for it because he can't look for it because his eyes…well, they're in that other part that he's looking for.

~ Big, Gargantuan & Ridiculously Oversized ~

Both the cities of Burwash Landing, Yukon, and Quesnel, BC, claim to have the "World's Largest Gold Pan." The Gold Rush was big in these here parts! The pan at Burwash Landing is 6.4 metres in diameter and the pan at Quesnel, sadly, is only 5.5 metres across. The Yukon wins out on this one! The Burwash Landing gold pan also sports a scenic painting of Kluane Lake and is located beside the Burwash Museum of Natural History at historic Mile 1093 (Kilometre 1759) on the Alaska Highway.

RAILWAY BRIDGE
WELLINGTON, PRINCE EDWARD ISLAND

A railway bridge west of Summerside, PEI, is the setting for an odd little East Coast mystery. On December evenings since 1885, a phantom train has often been seen crossing the bridge near Wellington. It's a train, so the bridge thing makes sense. I mean, a train in a lake would be really odd. People have reported seeing the chug-chug-chugging phantom engine with multiple railroad cars and even passengers at times when no trains were scheduled, none were running late and nothing named Via was in the area.

PLACES WHERE GHOSTS FROLIC IN THE GREAT OUTDOORS

CROWSNEST PASS
ALBERTA

The Crowsnest Pass is where the CPR crosses the Continental Divide from Alberta to BC. It's located in the Canadian Rockies at an elevation of 1357 metres. Weather can be, at times, extreme, and neighbours are few and far between in what can be a quiet and lonely area. It's a place of legend and lore.

They say that when the wind blows in "The Pass," Montie Lewis, the haunting hooker of Turtle Mountain, is out looking for her jewels…and perhaps still attempting to practise the world's oldest profession. A well-known turn of the century "lady-of-the-evening," Montie was also known for her great love of gems. Apparently she was always seen wearing jewels, whether she was dressed in clothing or frolicking about in the altogether!

Montie's bejewelled life took a tragic turn when she was found murdered. (That's got to be a drag!) She clearly learned the hard way that "you can't take it with you." However, evidence suggests that one of Montie's gentleman callers had just that in mind. He had a thing for Montie's precious gems—which does not refer to any particular part of her body. The lout offed poor Montie in the bed where she lay and then up and disappeared with her diamonds that day. Ya don't say.

So now, whenever the wind blows around Turtle Mountain, it's said that Montie's a-moanin'! I don't know. It seems a bit rude to suggest that a wind blowing across the pass is actually a hooker moaning over a trick gone bad!

~ Big, Gargantuan & Ridiculously Oversized ~

St. Claude, Manitoba, is a dairy community located an hour southwest of Winnipeg. The town has a rich French heritage, which is why "La Pipe" is located there. And just what is "La Pipe"? It's the "World's Largest Smokable Pipe." That's right, a very large pipe just like your grandfather used to smoke…not the water kind that your cousin Dave uses. And it was, indeed, built for smoking. If you've got enough tobacco and gigantic-sized lungs, I guess you could sit back with a newspaper and enjoy a puff. The pipe is 6 metres long and was built to commemorate early settlers who came from Jura, France, where the main industry was making pipes.

CANOE LAKE
ALGONQUIN PROVINCIAL PARK, ONTARIO

Algonquin Provincial Park is the second oldest provincial park in Canada. Established in 1893, the park covers 7723 km² —an area larger than Prince Edward Island. The vast park includes woodlands, lakes and rivers and is situated on the south edge of the Canadian Shield between Georgian Bay and the Ottawa River. Algonquin is remote, easy to get lost in and full of stories that include ghosts, murder and mystery.

And that's how we come to Tom Thompson. His death and what followed have become one of the best examples of Algonquin's mysterious lore.

The ghost of Tom Thomson haunts Canoe Lake in Algonquin Park. That's right! The late and venerated painter of the Canadian wilderness and affiliate of the Group of Seven— but not a member, because he, like Groucho Marx, would never join any group that would have him as a member…or something like that…

We all remember the story forced on us in history or art class where they talked about how old T.T. was an accomplished outdoorsman and talented painter, but somehow in 1917, turned up dead under his canoe with a gash on his head and fishing line wrapped around his ankle. I don't know about you, but I am clearly seeing an ironic Mister Bean–like moment that, if it weren't tragic, would actually be sitcom funny.

Anyway, since 1917, people claim to have seen a lone and ghostly figure paddling a canoe through the mist on Canoe Lake. So, he's kind of a benign haunter, because he doesn't say anything to anyone or scare them or even do a quick sketch that they could sell to the National Gallery for a fin or a million.

Explanations for his mysterious death include a love triangle gone wrong—oh, you know those artists! There's also some controversy surrounding the fact his family had him moved from his original burial site beside Canoe Lake to Heath, Ontario, with some other body showing up in his Canoe Lake grave in the 1950s.

CAMPOBELLO ISLAND
NEW BRUNSWICK

Campobello Island lies at the mouth of the Bay of Fundy, off the southeast coast of New Brunswick and the northeast tip of Maine. It is 16 kilometres long and only a couple of kilometres wide. Not the largest island you'll ever visit, but F.D.R. sure did like it. That's right—the island served as a retreat for U.S. President Franklin Delano Roosevelt. It also spouts a weird tale of haunting.

The haunter in question is known as "Bingo Man." On Monday nights, the ghost of this elderly man rises from his grave and treks down to the local bingo barn! No word on who he might be, whether he's ever yelled "Bingo!" or if he pursues time-honoured bingo rituals involving chachkas, coloured dabbers or green-haired gnome dolls

LITTLE LEPREAU BEACH
LEPREAU, NEW BRUNSWICK

Leapreau, New Brunswick, is a friendly little village south of Saint John. It's a place where you can get groceries, gas or a quick lunch. Nearby, there's a provincial park with a picnic area and the pride of the area, Lepreau Falls, where the Lepreau River meanders ever lower over flat rocks until it finally roars over a rocky ledge.

Nearby is Little Lepreau Beach. It may be picturesque during the day, but visiting the beach in the depths of darkness can be a scary experience. It starts with the sounds of chains rattling in the distance, but nothing can be seen. And if you hang around until morning, you may be lucky enough to see markings in the sand that look disturbingly like those of dragging chains and huge metal balls.

What does all this mean? What's the explanation? Well, this little stretch of Atlantic beach is said to be where people suffering from cholera during an epidemic were chained together and left to die, en masse, on the beach. And apparently, they still aren't happy about it and refuse to move out. They rattle their chains…from the grave! And smoosh the beach sand from there, as well.

~ Big, Gargantuan & Ridiculously Oversized ~

If you visit Duncan, BC, just north of Victoria on Vancouver Island, you will find yourself in the locale that possesses the "World's Largest Hockey Stick and Puck." The hockey stick is 62.5 metres long and is attached to the community centre. The Government of Canada commissioned this classic kitsch of Canadiana for Vancouver's Expo 86. After the Expo ended, the stick was floated by barge from Vancouver to Duncan. No word on how the puck got there, but my hope is that it was a slapshot from the DEW Line.

~ Big, Gargantuan & Ridiculously Oversized ~

The town of Porcupine Plain, Saskatchewan, east of Saskatoon, is home to (what else?) the "World's Largest Porcupine." The town's mascot stands in a roadside park atop a wooden platform with his name on it. He's called Quilly Willy, and according to the town's web site, Quilly Willy "represents the genuine welcome all residents of Porcupine Plain extend to its visitors." Quilly Willy is nearly 4 metres tall, so let's hope his genuine welcome doesn't involve a prickly hug.

BASTION SQUARE
VICTORIA, BRITISH COLUMBIA

Bastion Square is the site of the original Fort Victoria. It's located in the heart of British Columbia's capital city. Many small shops, arts and crafts stands and restaurants frame the square. It also has several benches for catching the great view of the inner harbour, or if you're lucky, a ghost. That's right, ice cream and postcards and sprites, oh my!

Bastion Square is often called the most haunted spot in Canada's most haunted city. In Victoria's not-so-distant past, a jail was situated in the square, where executions actually took place, And, I guess, some of the executed are a little peeved at their fate, so they won't leave and like to play a little "scare the living" game.

People claim to have heard the sounds of rattling chains and are then confronted by the ghostly apparition of a man dressed in a prison uniform—black and white stripes and all. He may have been killed on his way to being executed by a prison guard who thought he wasn't moving quickly enough. And so he wanders Bastion Square today looking for justice…or the gallows, so he can be executed all proper-like.

So, if you're in the vicinity, visit Bastion Square, where you can eat, drink and be merry because you aren't a ghost!

~ Big, Gargantuan & Ridiculously Oversized ~

The "World's Largest Tin Soldier" is located at New Westminster Quay in the Vancouver-area city of New Westminster, BC. It stands almost 10 metres high and weighs in at a portly 5 tonnes—though I understand most of that is water weight. Weight Watchers has been contacted and the steel Gomer Pyle is being put on strict diet. The soldier was modelled on the Royal Engineers who founded the city of New Westminster back in 1859. He's got a bright red coat, yellow belt and black pants, and was unveiled at the Royal Westminster Regiment Armoury in July 2000. Workers and management of the BC Sheet Metal Industry built the soldier in support of the Simon Fraser Society for Community Living and their programs for children with special needs. When the big guy was moved to his permanent home at Westminster Quay, a time capsule was added, which will be opened in 2025. Gosh, I wonder if there are tin soldier accessories in it? Maybe a tin horse or a tin riding crop or maybe a big metal key they can use to wind the soldier up so he can dance a jaunty Royal Engineers jig?

Lakes and Bays and their Soggy Inhabitants

People who go to sea in ships and out on lakes in boats and generally swim and splash and float on Canadian waters...should look out!

There are mysterious creatures great and small that will scare you, rub up against you in a suggestive manner and generally make you look foolish talking about them on TV. They may even eat you or part of your dinghy. Who knew Canada had such a rich quantity of unknown, mysterious and slightly shy aquatic life that may have resided here even longer than our First Nations peoples.

British Columbia captures the title of "Sea Serpent Capital" with the creepiest waters and the most famous of these large, but shy, overgrown denizens of the deep.

OKANAGAN LAKE
BRITISH COLUMBIA

Okanagan Lake is found in one of the most beautiful regions of what is arguably the most beautiful part of Canada. Located in south-central British Columbia, Okanagan Lake is deep, long (155 kilometres) and relatively narrow. It's also the largest of the five main and interconnected lakes in the region. The area is known for its numerous sunny days, beautiful beaches and agriculture, and is one of the most abundant fruit- and wine-growing regions of the country. Hiking, biking, sailing, golf and skiing are enjoyed by residents and the tourists who flock to the area's many resorts. Sounds like the perfect place, doesn't it? But in truth, not so perfect, for a monster resides in Okanagan Lake, and he's a publicity hound.

> *The legend lives on from the Salish on down*
> *Of the deep lake they call Okanagan*
> *The monster was the pride of the demonic side*
> *And Squally Point was the place where they'd feed him...*

Now, just how famous would Okanagan Lake's monster be if Gordon Lightfoot had penned these lyrics instead of the ones about that sinking ship? I would guess probably not a lot more famous than he is today. That's because, since the 1920s, the people of this fine region have promoted the heck out of Ogopogo.

Before modern day promotion however, local Natives knew the "snake in the lake" as N'ha-A-Itk. Representations of the many-humped creature go back to pre-contact petroglyphs. The Natives also identified the creature's home specifically as the caves beneath Squally Point, and when they were out canoeing in the area, they would drop sacrifices to him in the form of chickens or pigs. Somehow the drowning of a small animal proved to them the existence of the beast.

Fast forward to 1926, when sharp local promoters latched on to an old dancehall song about the lake's serpent and rechristened the creature "Ogopogo." The BC government even got in on the Ogopogo ride that year, announcing that the new ferry being constructed for the lake would have monster-repelling devices. Later, they even put up a sign officially naming Squally Point Ogopogo's home.

Ogopogo is generally reported to be green, but he has also appeared as dark blue, black or brown. With those muted tones, he's either a fashion-conscious enigma or a true water chameleon. He's somewhere between 4.5 and 25 metres long, has numerous humps and reportedly moves at an astounding speed in an undulating motion. His head is shaped either like that of a horse or a reptile. These descriptions led a British zoologist to speculate that Ogopogo is a primitive serpentine whale of the genus *Zeuglodon*.

Ogopogo sightings are numerous, officially dating back to 1872, and continue right up to today. One of the most intriguing of those sightings involves a man swimming the length of the lake

to raise money for cancer. He claims that two Ogopogos swam underneath him for two hours. He was frightened and got out of the water. He continued his swim some time later, and the Ogopogos were apparently waiting for him like a loyal set of dogs. I guess the benign creatures like to support a good cause.

Over the years there have been sightings by "reputable" individuals as well as small and large groups of people. Ogopogo has been seen "frolicking," "chasing his tail" and "sunning himself on the beach." These are, coincidentally, the major recreational activities associated with the lake. Ogopogo has also been mistaken for a log, a sturgeon and even a beaver…or perhaps with enough alcohol, it's the other way around.

Most recently, a group of local businessmen offered a $2 million prize for proof of Ogopogo's existence. Disappointingly, no definitive proof was found, and the prize went unclaimed. There are, however, many blurred photos, inconclusive videos, and let's not forget the investigations by TV's *Unsolved Mysteries*, *Inside Edition* and the Japanese media.

CADBORO BAY
VICTORIA, BRITISH COLUMBIA

Cadboro Bay, British Columbia, is located within the Municipality of Saanich, which is part of the Greater Victoria area. The area has a Mediterranean-like climate, with warm, sunny summers and moderately wet winters. It's scenic, residential and adjacent to the University of Victoria. The bay is also known for its soggy and mysterious resident.

That's right, sleepy little Cadboro Bay is where you'll find the home of "Caddy," the saltwater counterpart to Okanagan Lake's Ogopogo. In 1933, *Victoria Times* newspaper editor, Archie Willis, latched on to the sea serpent as a local mascot and dubbed him "Cadborosaurus." The creature quickly became known by the shorter and much more adorable name "Caddy."

Caddy's emergence as mascot and "terror" came a scant seven years after Ogopogo's star took off. Mysterious coincidence or copycat marketing scheme? You be the judge.

Caddy has two large flippers and either a mane or a jagged crest. His head is either horse-shaped or camel-like, and like all sea serpents, he is long (up to 30 metres) and thin and moves at incredible speeds in an undulating motion. He has either a scary or a dopey face, depending on the sighting report...or is that the sighting reporter?

Caddy has a couple of legs up (though no actual legs) on Ogopogo in that he has a much smaller mate who goes by the equally adorable name "Amy." He's also been seriously studied by at least two scientists: Paul LeBlond from the University of British Columbia and E.L. Bousfield from the Royal British Columbia Museum. The pair gave Caddy his scientific name, *Cadborosaurus willsi*. Bousfield went so far as to notify the American Society of Zoologists that Caddy actually existed. Bet that was an interesting conversation: "A what? Who is this?"

Although Cadboro Bay is the designated home of Caddy, he has been seen up and down the coast of Vancouver Island. The similarities between Ogopogo and Caddy are so numerous that my personal theory is that they are one and the same. I will even go so far as to suggest that Ogopogo, like many other retirees, has chosen to spend his golden years in Victoria under an assumed name.

~ Big, Gargantuan & Ridiculously Oversized ~

The municipality of Moonbeam, Ontario, has built (what else?) a flying saucer as a town landmark. Get it? Moonbeam...flying saucer? Located in Moonbeam's major town of New Liskeard, the flying saucer doesn't actually fly—it's anchored to the ground. The saucer is 5.5 metres in diameter, 2.7 metres tall and has rotating flashing lights on its saucer edges, just like the real ones.

LAKE CHAMPLAIN
QUÉBEC

Often called "America's Loch Ness," Lake Champlain lies partly in Québec, partly in New York State and partly in Vermont. The lake is 200 kilometres long and quite deep, just like Loch Ness. Lake Champlain also has a monster. This one is lovably (and not terribly creatively) called "Champ."

Champ has been sighted more than 240 times. He's dark in colour, has a long neck, a couple of humps and may be as much as 8 metres long. He's probably a plesiosaur… Notice any similarities here?

As with all of our aliens of the waters, there are many photographs that prove very little. However, in 1977, a Connecticut woman named Sandra Mansi caught Champ sunning himself and snapped a very good photo with her Kodak Instamatic (remember those cameras?). Scientists studied the picture and declared it hadn't been retouched. The photo drew a lot of attention and even appeared in *Time* magazine on July 13, 1981.

There are have also been at least two scientific soundings done on the lake that showed something was there. No word on what that "something" was nor whether that which lies below the surface of Lake Champlain is considered intelligent…

~ Big, Gargantuan & Ridiculously Oversized ~

The "World's Largest Moose" stands next to the Trans-Canada Highway at the Moose Jaw Visitors Centre in Saskatchewan. He's named Mac after the late Moose Jaw alderman, Les McKenzie. Mac, the moose, not the alderman, stands nearly 10 metres tall and weighs in at a gargantuan 9000 kilograms. At that size, you must be able to see him as far away as Winnipeg.

LAC MEMPHRÉMAGOG
QUÉBEC

Lake Memphrémagog is 100 kilometres east of Montréal near Sherbrooke, Québec, and crosses the border into Vermont. The lake is 40 kilometres long, finger-like and nestled between mountains. It's a deep, cold, freshwater lake that contains another of Québec's weird lake creatures, "Memphré."

Memphré resembles Ogopogo in most respects. Memphré's got the long neck, the humps and the horse face, as well as the undulating motion and the shyness about having his picture taken.

The first European settlers encountered local First Nations people, who reportedly wouldn't swim in the lake because they were afraid of the monster. Since then, there have been well over 200 sightings, dating back to the 1800s. The local expert on the subject is a man named Jacques Boisvert. He founded an organization to study Memphré called the International Dracontology Society. He's collected much anecdotal evidence, but nothing conclusive. Darn, I thought maybe this time we had one!

If you're in the area and looking to waste some time looking for Memphré, he's said to make his home in a cave at the base of Owl's Head Mountain. Good luck!

LAKE POHÉNÉGAMOOK
QUÉBEC

Lake Pohénégamook is 60 kilometres south of Rivière-du-Loup and 250 kilometres from Québec City. It lies just north of the Québec–Maine border. The lake is 11 kilometres long and takes its name from a First Nations word meaning "mocking"…Now, we're talking!

La bête du lac (the beast of the lake) goes by the name "Ponik." Unlike the other two Québec lake monsters, Champ and Memphré, Ponik is 100% Québecois. No cross-border Yankee serpent trash here!

Ponik, though, has seen better days. The heyday for sighting reports really peaked back in 1957 and 1958. In 1957, Ponik startled a local abbé, Leopold Plante, while he was fishing, and the abbé began promoting the existence of the creature. He said Ponik looked like "a long overturned canoe crossing the lake, leaving a wake behind."

Ponik has also been variously described as being black or brown, hairless and having some sort of "crenellation" in the middle of his back. The standard serpentine body, two to three humps, flippers and horse head have also been mentioned previously. He's also said to be about 10 metres long.

A number of studies of have been carried out, but no official study has produced evidence of a creature living in the lake. This hasn't, however, stopped the speculation about Ponik's existence or that he might actually be some form of sturgeon, plesiosaur or a giant and ancient snake.

TURTLE LAKE
SASKATCHEWAN

Turtle Lake is located in west-central Saskatchewan, 120 kilometres northwest of North Battleford and about a two-and-a-half-hour drive from Saskatoon. It's not a densely populated area, at least by human standards. The area is known for its recreational activities such as boating, fishing and golfing. The lake got its quaint name because someone thought it looked like a turtle. There are no turtles in Turtle Lake, but there are fish. Which is a good thing, because lake monsters need something to eat. And, as the theme of this chapter implies—you guessed it— there is a monster in Turtle Lake.

Tales of the monster go back to First Nations people. Their legends speak of a terror in Turtle Lake and say that people who entered his territory were never seen again.

There have been numerous sightings of the lake creature over the last 40 or more years. He's described as smooth...or scaly...with a dorsal fin...or without a dorsal fin...and his head resembles a dog...or a seahorse...or a pig. So, with this pinpoint accuracy, he could be either a plesiosaur or one of my half-cousins twice removed. He also has the requisite earth-tone coloration.

Sadly, this poor lake serpent does not have a kitschy name like Ogopogo or Champ! Perhaps a catchy name contest will eventually be had and the "Terror of Turtle Lake" will get what's coming to him, and more t-shirts can be mass-produced and sold!

~ Big, Gargantuan & Ridiculously Oversized ~

The "World's Largest Grasshopper" is located in the farming town of Wilkie, Saskatchewan, 160 kilometres west of Saskatoon. It's made of cedar, painted brown and green, and is 5.5 metres long and 1.8 metres wide. The Wilkie grasshopper was designed by local artist Byron Hansen and is based on smaller versions of grasshoppers that he is well known for making.

LAKE MANITOBA
MANITOBA

Lake Manitoba is a 200-kilometre-long, irregularly shaped lake that lies northwest of Winnipeg. It has marshy shores and is fed from Lake Winnipegosis, eventually draining into Lake Winnipeg. Winnipeg, Winnipegosis? Looks like someone was coasting when they were naming Manitoba's lakes.

Lake Manitoba is home to "Manipogo," another lake serpent very similar in size, shape and blah, blah, blah to Ogopogo (still king!). In fact, there have been reports of "animals of unclassi-fied type" not only in Lake Manitoba, but also in Lakes Winnipeg, Winnipegosis, Dauphin, Cedar and Dirty. Speculation has been that Manipogo travels throughout the Manitoba lake system. And why not, if you've got flippers and frequent serpent miles to spare!

The most intriguing story of the elusive Manipogo involves a hoax perpetrated in 1997. The media were informed that Manipogo had been captured, killed and put up for auction by a Manitoba farmer who wanted $200,000 for it. The story quickly unravelled when the local RCMP denied that they had seen or heard any-thing about it. However, that did not stop various news organiza-tions from running the story as though it was gospel.

~ Big, Gargantuan & Ridiculously Oversized ~

As you enter the town of Watson, Saskatchewan, you'll be greeted by a 7.6-metre-tall statue of Santa Claus, his right arm outstretched as if waving to you. Be polite and wave back! Watson claims to be the home of the original "Santa Claus Day," which continues to be commemorated in Watson and other copycat communities to this day. Thus, the statue is clearly apropos!

LAKE SIMCOE
ONTARIO

Lake Simcoe is an hour's drive north of Toronto. It's an oval-shaped lake with a couple of irregular fingers that jut out north, south and west. The major city on Lake Simcoe is Barrie. The lake is known for offering much recreational activity and has a scary little secret—there's a lake monster there that, depending on where he's seen, goes either by the name "Igopogo" or "Kempenfelt Kelly." Doesn't it just figure that Ontario needs two names for a creature, whereas other provinces can make do with just one?

Igopogo is, of course, a direct ripoff of Ogopogo. Kempenfelt Kelly gets his name from Kempenfelt Bay, a place on the north-west side of the lake, where the creature has often been spotted. The creature resembles Ogopogo in every respect except one—he's actually quite tiny. Igopogo Kelly has been described as being no more than 3.5 metres long.

Igopogofelt seems to move at a much more leisurely pace than other lake monsters. He's got a sense of humour, though, since many sightings involve him startling picnickers or sneaking up on unsuspecting boaters. And alcohol, I'm sure, had nothing to do with any of the encounters.

There's been speculation that Igofeltpogo Kelly is more mammalian than serpent-like. Infrequent sightings have also raised the possibility that IgoKelly-PogoFelt has passed on.

~ Big, Gargantuan & Ridiculously Oversized ~

The town of Baie-Comeau, Québec, has a life-sized statue of a man paddling a canoe. The statue doesn't represent Cartier or Champlain or even one of those *coureurs de bois*. It actually represents the town's founder, Colonel Robert McCormick, who was also the owner of the *Chicago Tribune* newspaper. The statue was erected in 1956, a year after the colonel passed away. Other "big" sites in the area are Manic-5, the world's largest multiple-arch and buttress dam, and Manic-2, the world's largest hollow-joint gravity dam. Baie-Comeau is also famous for being the hometown of Canada's former larger-than-life prime minister—Brian Mulroney.

LAKE UTOPIA
NEW BRUNSWICK

Lake Utopia is in southwestern New Brunswick, not far from the Bay of Fundy and northeast of St. George. The lake is 8 kilometres long and 3 kilometres wide and drains into the Magaguadavic River. The river was named by local First Nations tribes and may mean "River of Eels." Ominous, no? *Mais oui!* (Nice to be able to use my high-school French!)

According to one researcher, naming the river Magaguadavic apparently helps prove the existence of Lake Utopia's monster, since eels spawn at sea but return to their native lakes to live. That's what's been suggested to explain the existence of Lake Utopia's monster.

Just like Saskatchewan's Turtle Lake monster, there's been no catchy moniker attached to this one in Lake Utopia...no Utopia Tom or Uta of Utopia or even Kyle. That may be because sightings have been less frequent than some of the other serpentine lake denizens—on average only every three to five years.

There's a strange Native legend about the Lake Utopia monster chasing a canoe with its huge jaws snapping and another about it breaking through the surface ice of the frozen lake. However, like many of the other lake monsters, Utopia's is most often reported as being rather playful and docile and is most often seen sunning himself. Yep, another lazy-ass monster that likes to suntan!

For the sceptics among you, you'll be glad to hear that sceptical *Enquirer Magazine* investigated the lake. The results—they're sceptical! Actually, they're sure there's nothing there. Which I guess isn't much of a surprise coming from sceptics. As for the believers, they still believe. Good for you!

CAPE BRETON ISLAND
NOVA SCOTIA

Cape Breton is a beautiful island linked to the rest of Nova Scotia by a causeway. It's known for its friendly people, windswept coastline and majestic mountain ranges. As with many maritime communities across the globe, strange stories of the sea are ingrained.

Stories of sea serpents and lake monsters in this area have been reported for hundreds of years. There may be some eel-type monster in Lake Ainslie, for instance, but no name has been attached to it nor any marketing budget allotted to promote it.

Fishermen have been reporting encounters with strange creatures for centuries. The most recent seems to have occurred in 2003, in the cove off Point Aconi. A lobster fisherman claims to have had an encounter with a creature he thought at first was a big log. Oh, that old ruse! But it turned out to have a snake-like body, a turtle's head, smooth skin, brown coloration and was about 8 metres long. Although wary of the creature at first, the fisherman followed it for some time. The creature allegedly raised its head out of the water several times during the soggy surveillance.

The Nova Scotia Museum of Natural History couldn't say for sure what the creature was, but suggested it could be an oarfish. Oarfish have ribbon-like bodies and usually grow to 8 metres in length. Cryptozoologists debunked the explanation calling it, well…bunk. The Nova Scotia Museum of Natural History recanted, and everyone agreed they didn't know what it was. Talk about getting along. Those people on the East Coast really are friendly!

AND THE REST OF THE WEIRD AND SOGGY PLACES…

There have also been sightings of various "unexplained creatures" off the Grand Banks in Newfoundland, in Lake Erie at Kingston, Ontario (where they call him "Kingstie"), at Harrison Lake in BC, and even perhaps in Saddle Lake, Alberta. What a mosaic of a country this is!

~ Big, Gargantuan & Ridiculously Oversized ~

You'll see dinosaurs overlooking a group of small islands at the entrance to the Manicouagan Peninsula in the municipality of Ragueneau, Québec. There's a "mama" dinosaur and a "baby" dinosaur but no "papa" dinosaur. So, what gives? Is this scene a harmless bit of roadside fun or a commentary on the modern fractured family? *Mon dieu! Ce n'est pas possible!*

Interplanetary Kraft, Neither Orange Nor Individually Wrapped

One of the most fascinating subjects for me has always been anything and everything to do with UFOs, abductions and aliens. As I already mentioned in my introduction, I did, in fact, see a UFO when I was a kid. I admit it is much more a fuzzy, kid-remembered image than a solid, discernible and provable fact, but such is the stuff that the UFO phenomenon is based on.

I have studied so much UFO literature—from books to the wackiest of Internet web sites. I even once had an e-mail correspondence with an American woman who claimed to be in contact with 12 different alien races— we're talking interplanetary aliens, not the illegal types that Americans normally talk about.

Over the years, the hype, the hardcore believers and converted masses have all pushed me more towards scepticism than to belief. This is why I have, oh so cleverly, titled this chapter "Interplanetary Kraft, Neither Orange Nor ☞

Individually Wrapped." For those individually wrapped pieces of glow-in-the-dark cheese could as easily be UFOs or sites of alien abduction as most of the thousands of sighting/abduction reports filed in Canada each year.

Weird Canadian places that are related to UFOs are elusive. UFO sightings happen all over the place, in every region of the country and rarely in the same place twice. This makes my task difficult. If you want to see UFOs, apparently they most often hang out at nuclear power facilities or military installations. With the number of military bases dwindling, it becomes far more difficult to see them there year after year. However, with power consumption increasing and nuclear power production growing, it seems to me that's where to look.

I have included a couple of places in this section that count as weird UFO sighting places: Shirley's Bay, Shag Harbour and Falcon Lake. However, head for the nukes and you'll be in weird country. As well, some conveniently provided UFO sighting areas have been designated and funded by various levels of government, including St. Paul, Alberta, with its UFO Landing Pad, and Vulcan, Alberta, where a replica Starship Enterprise will welcome alien visitors of the extra-Alberta kind and the extraterrestrial kind alike.

Let's face it, the UFO thing used to be a dirty little secret, barely talked about in serious conversation and relegated to off-colour ☞

jokes and snickers behind the whackos' backs. But that is no more. The whole thing has developed from a niche market into a huge industry. And give the province of Alberta credit here, when the rest of us were still laughing, they were embracing the phenomenon full on.

Oh, and there's one more likelihood for seeing those elusive UFOs. If you live in the middle of nowhere, are out tipping cows and your name is Bob, you're bound to see one. Perhaps you'll even get to appear on Canada AM. *Good luck, Bob!*

PLACES TO HAVE FUN WITH UFOS

UFO LANDING PAD
ST. PAUL, ALBERTA

This, in fact, is no joke. No, really. In 1967, as one of Canada's centennial projects, the town of St. Paul, Alberta, built a landing pad for extraterrestrial and UFO visitors to our planet. I repeat: this is no joke!

In the mid-1960s, the Government of Canada encouraged all Canadian communities to undertake centennial projects to commemorate Canada's first 100 years. St. Paul put many projects in the works, but the one that garnered the most attention, and still does, is the UFO Landing Pad.

The idea for the pad actually came from W.R. Treleaven of Hamilton, Ontario, and Ken Reed of Calgary. And they actually convinced Alberta's lieutenant-governor, the Honourable Grant MacEwan, to turn the sod at the inauguration ceremony.

The round, 118-tonne pad is made out of concrete and steel and includes six 76-centimetre pylons that form the main column. It is raised above the ground and stands out…well, as a landing pad. A map of Canada, made of stones donated by each Canadian province, is embossed on the landing pad's backstop, and provincial flags are flown atop the backstop.

When the project was originally built, a time capsule was sealed into the backstop with letters addressed to Canadians from the likes of Ernest Manning. The time capsule will remain sealed until 2067, Canada's bicentennial. That will surely be an interesting "opening" ceremony.

The whole pad was completed and unveiled on June 3, 1967. Canada's Minister of Defence, Paul Hellyer, flew in by helicopter to officially open the pad. It was a joyful and wacky time, no doubt.

A sign beside the pad reads as follows: "Republic of St. Paul (Stargate Alpha). The area under the World's First UFO Landing Pad was designated international by the Town of St. Paul as a symbol of our faith that mankind will maintain the outer universe free from national wars and strife. That future travel in space will be safe for all intergalactic beings, all visitors from earth or otherwise are welcome to this territory and to the Town of St. Paul."

But St. Paul hasn't rested on its 1967 laurels. In 1993, they built a saucer-shaped structure beside the pad to serve as a tourist information booth. Then in 1996, they built an addition to the booth to house a UFO Interpretive display. The display shows actual (?) photographs of UFOs, crop circles and cattle mutilations, among other things. It also explains the various degrees of sighting reports (Close Encounter of the First Kind, Second Kind, Third Kind, etc.).

Along with the interpretive centre, the town also created and mans a toll-free UFO sighting hotline. The number is 1-888-SEE-UFOS (733-8367), for anyone who has something to report. The hotline has received reports on UFO sightings, cattle mutilations, crop circles, abductions and encounters of all kinds.

And we're not quite finished yet. St. Paul's UFO Landing Pad has attracted attention from all over the world. In fact, two of the most famous visitors to the pad were Queen Elizabeth II and the late Mother Theresa. However, there still haven't been any intergalactic visitors, though the town's collective fingers are crossed.

St. Paul is located in Alberta's Lakeland region, approximately 200 kilometres northeast of Edmonton.

~ Big, Gargantuan & Ridiculously Oversized ~

The "World's Largest Pair of Cross-Country Skis" (with poles) is located in the BC Interior town of 100 Mile House. The skis are 12 metres long and the poles are 9 metres long. They were commissioned by the ski manufacturer Karhu and dedicated by the Man-in-Motion himself, Rick Hansen, way back in 1987. The skis are located in front of the Visitor Infocentre on the west side of Highway 97. The town is also known for successfully fighting the federal government to keep their town's name from being metrically converted to 160.9344 Kilometre House. I mean, really!

VULCAN TOURISM AND TREK STATION
VULCAN, ALBERTA

Vulcan is, of course, the birth planet of *Star Trek*'s Mr. Spock. Vulcan, Alberta, is of course, yet another Alberta town that knows how to have fun and capitalize on its name in connection with a defunct, but highly popular TV show! And I say: Way to go! Or live long and prosper. And from the look of things, Vulcan will.

Vulcan has long been a farming community. The area was actually surveyed in 1910, so the town had its name long before *Star Trek* ever existed. However, it wasn't until 1998 that the Vulcan Tourism and Trek Station opened, so the question is, who is capitalizing on what's fame?

The Tourism and Trek Centre consists of a main building, which was designed to look like a landing spaceship, and the replica *Star Trek*-like starship. They've put some nifty fibre optic lighting on the centre's soffits to enhance the idea of the landing spaceship. Inside the tourism centre, the captain and the ever-friendly crew greet each and every visitor.

The tourism centre boasts *Star Trek*-related displays and a replica *Starship Enterprise* main bridge, where people can dress up in *Star Trek* costumes and have their photos taken with cardboard cutouts of *Star Trek* cast members. You can also obtain tourism information and maps of Vulcan and Vulcan County. How odd!

Clearly one of the highlights of the Tourism and Trek Centre is the replica *Starship Enterprise*. The starship is 9.4 metres long and sports the insignia "FX6 -1995-A." "FX6" is the identifier of Vulcan's airports, 1995 is the year the ship was unveiled and "A" designates the first project launched under the Science and Trek theme.

Each June, the town hosts the annual Galaxyfest and Spockdays Festival. The two events used to be separate, but I guess Starfleet can only sponsor so many events in a single green-blooded town. Last year, the actors from the *Star Trek: The Next Generation* TV show, the Klingons Gowron and Martock (Robert O'Reilly and J.G. Hertzler), were the festival's guest speakers. Apparently they killed the crowd with their version of a Klingon hip-hop song. They also answered questions from the hundreds of fans dressed as Romulans, Borg, Klingons and Ferengi. Must have been a sight for sore Betazoid eyes to see. Galaxyfest events also include fireworks (phaser fireworks, I'm guessing), bed races, an art walk and a parade.

If you want to visit the Vulcan Tourism and Trek Centre, beam yourself over to Vulcan. Better yet, drive the hour or so from either Calgary or Lethbridge. Starfleet awaits you!

PLACES FOR THE SERIOUS UFO NUT

THE WORLD'S FIRST FLYING SAUCER SIGHTING STATION
SHIRLEY'S BAY, ONTARIO

In the 1950s, the Canadian government was apparently not afraid to say that it was looking for UFOs. In fact, the government, under the guidance of the eminently respected Wilbert Smith and the Department of Transport, was not even afraid to say they'd set up the world's first officially sponsored Saucer Sighting Station, just 16 kilometres outside Ottawa in the community of Shirley's Bay. The program started in 1952 and ran for more than three and half years.

The Saucer Sighting Station was housed in a 3.6-metre square shack. It wasn't manned, but it was linked by some form of alarm system to a fully manned ionospheric station nearby. Inside the sighting station was expensive and complex equipment able to detect radio noise, magnetic fluctuations and gamma rays.

At one point in 1954, station personnel detected what they thought was a flying saucer. The bells and alarms apparently went off, and Smith and others ran outside to see what they could see. Nothing, as it turned out, because the whole area was fogged in. But this didn't stop Smith from announcing to the press that he thought he'd caught one. He was quickly reprimanded, and the project was officially shut down within the month. It was an ignominious end, to say the least. However, Shirley's Bay will always have the distinction of being the site of the world's first flying saucer sighting station.

~ Big, Gargantuan & Ridiculously Oversized ~

Pemmican Pete has been the ubiquitous mascot of Regina's summer exhibition, "Buffalo Days," since the mid-1960s. Pete is a buffalo
hunter clad in buckskins. He sports a beard and carries a rifle and
is most often seen sitting astride a giant buffalo. What else would
a buffalo hunter be doing? The Buffalo Days people had four replica
mascots built and positioned around Regina's exhibition grounds.
The 2.4-metre-tall Pemmican Pete rides his 2.1-metre-tall buffalo
buddy who's stuck on a really tall pole. When one of the original
mascots was damaged, Pete was removed and brought down from
his high post over the grounds, and people began dressing up as
Pemmican Pete and sitting astride the buffalo to have their pictures
taken. That's how the "real life" Pemmican Pete was discovered back
in the 1970s. Rollie Bourassa, one of Buffalo Days' founders, discovered a buckskin-clad fellow named Tom Doucette. Doucette was
apparently the spitting image of the mascot and went on to play
the real-life Pemmican Pete throughout the '70s, '80s and '90s.

CANADA'S ROSWELL
SHAG HARBOUR, NOVA SCOTIA

In UFO circles, the Shag Harbour incident is about as close as Canada gets to a Roswell-like incident. It involves the apparent crash of a UFO, many witnesses, government and military investigation, surveillance and strange and odd smells, sights and sounds.

The whole thing began on the night of October 4, 1967, above the waters of Shag Harbour, Nova Scotia. Shag Harbour was, and still is, a tiny fishing village at the southern tip of Nova Scotia. Just after 11:00 PM, witnesses claim to have noticed strange orange lights above the water that may or may not have numbered four and flashed in sequence. Sounds a bit like a Spielberg movie, if you ask me.

At some point, the lights turned at a 45-degree angle and dove towards the water. There may have then been a bright flash and an explosion. But whatever happened at that point, many people called the RCMP detachment at Barrington Passage to report the incident. The incident report refers only to the crash of a large aircraft into the harbour. The subject of UFOs apparently never came up.

Three officers were dispatched to the area. When the officers arrived at the shore near the crash site, they could still see the UFO with its bright yellow lights floating on the surface of the water. Apparently it was 18.3 metres in diameter and trailed some sort of yellow foam behind it on the surface of the water. It also gave off the distinctive odour of sulphur.

When government agencies and the military were asked if one of their aircraft was missing, the answer was no. Boats tried to reach the crash site, but by the time they did, the UFO had submerged and the lights had gone out. Some foam remained, however.

The next day the Canadian military sent the HMCS *Granby* to investigate. Divers spent four days in search of "something," but found nothing. And this is where the myth and folklore explode.

The whole incident was basically forgotten until the 1990s, when it took on mythic proportions and additions to the story emerged. Those additions involve underwater surveillance of the UFO over a 40-kilometre trek, a second UFO and the eventual escape of the otherworldly craft from the ocean depths. They also involve cover-up, trailing of witnesses and more murky yellow foam. Well, not more, but the whole thing might as well be covered in it.

So, if you're on Nova Scotia's south shore, have a look out over Shag Harbour. Lots of other people have.

FALCON LAKE
MANITOBA

The year 1967 seems to be a big one for weird Canadian UFO-related places. Clusters happen, I guess. Despite my scepticism and love of a laugh, there's something about the Falcon Lake incident that is both intriguing and has the ring of truth to it. Or at least it does to me.

Falcon Lake is east of Winnipeg, almost at the border of northern Ontario. On May 20, 1967, an amateur prospector from Winnipeg named Stephen Michalak found himself prospecting in Whiteshell Provincial Park. A flock of geese alerted him to the skies, where he spied two UFOs. One of the UFOs landed, while the other hovered for a time before departing the scene.

Michalak was both intrigued and a bit scared, so he stayed back for a time, sketching what he was seeing. He eventually approached the UFO and even heard voices from an open doorway, so he looked inside. However, his actions must have spooked the UFO's inhabitants, because the next thing he knew, the UFO turned, moved and sped off. But in its haste to depart, the UFO let blast go a blast of exhaust, which hit Michalak in the chest, setting his clothing on fire and leaving him with a large mark. He was forced to remove his burning clothes and suffered painful burns and illness.

Eventually, Michalak made his way back to the town of Falcon Lake and back to his home in Winnipeg, where he was treated for his burns and sickness. The RCMP got involved, interviewing Michalak several times. Tests on soil samples and Michalak's clothing came back with the result that the soil and clothes were radioactive. Well, that's weird.

And when Michalak finally took the RCMP to the landing site, they noted a semicircular barren spot, 14.6-metres in diameter, from which the naturally growing moss had some-how been removed.

The Department of National Defence marked the case "unsolved." So, this makes Falcon Lake a true government-certified weird place.

~ Big, Gargantuan & Ridiculously Oversized ~

The "World's Largest Fire Hydrant" is located in the town of Elm Creek, Manitoba, next to the fire hall. At 9 metres tall, it's more than just a kitschy photo-op for the practical people of Elm Creek—the hydrant is actually the town's water tank. For years, there have been plans to build a giant dog beside the fire hydrant, but nothing has appeared so far. I'm keeping my fingers crossed for them, though!

Odd, Mysterious or on the Verge of Being Offensive

Oddities, mysteries and offensive finds, lions and tigers and bears, oh my! No animals, actually. But these utterly odd Canadian splunks are the things that dreams—or nightmares—are made of. Splunks, by the way, are places where you'll find odd, mysterious and possibly offensive stuff. The word is new and was created by me, but I predict it will soon be listed in Canadian dictionaries…

Anyway, Sam Spade may have had the mystery of the Maltese Falcon, but he never got to consider the oddities of root cellars, gopher holes or a horsehair-padded dance floor. Sam missed out on the secrets of the Hammer of Thor and mystery rocks in Saskatchewan. And the "Spademan" never got to consider Saskatchewan's "Land of Rape and Honey" or outhouse racing—that's not racing to an outhouse, we're talking the actual racing of an outhouse. ☞

It's all here—the oddest of the odd, the most mysterious of mysteries and that thing that might offend.

And how offensive might it be to learn that secret midnight flights by the CIA are passing through a Canadian airport? We're talking terrorism suspects, no warrants and covert ops.

Who said Canadians are cold and staid and conservative? This little chapter should prove that statement wrong once and for all!

THE ODD

THE GOPHER HOLE MUSEUM
TORRINGTON, ALBERTA

In 1996, odd little Alberta (I mean that in the best possible way), opened yet another odd little attraction—the Gopher Hole Museum. The Gopher Hole Museum isn't so much a museum celebrating gopher holes, as it is a reason for someone to dress up dead gophers in costumes and pose them in a bunch of quaint little scenes. Each scene is considered a "hole." Thus, it's the Gopher Hole Museum. Get it?

Another redirection is in order here. The gophers are actually Richardson's ground squirrels, but I'm from the city, so you could tell me they are goldfish, and I'd believe you. The gopher hole scenes include: the Royal Canadian Mounted Gopher, a Gophersmith, the Reverend Gopher, a Gopher Hairdresser, Olympic Gophers and oh, so many more.

Torrington's Gopher Hole Museum has generated a great deal of controversy. Some people are apparently offended by the fact that the museum uses real, non-living gophers in their displays. Since before the museum opened, the People for the Ethical Treatment of Animals (PETA) have been urging the Gopher Hole Museum to use fake gophers instead.

The town and the museum have seen no reason to honour PETA's request. The town has huge problems with the beasts and has to off them anyhow. So, why not use what's leftover and put it on display? Or even create a silly tourist attraction. You could say it's a case of turning vinegar into wine, a negative into a positive (or road kill into a furry priest?). Anyway, the controversy probably won't soon die down, and the museum is thriving. Thanks to PETA, the museum has attracted international media attention and visitors from all over the world. You have to admit it's a pretty successful little endeavour for a minor amount of government grant money. Every little community should be so fortunate to garner such publicity and tourists.

When you visit Torrrington—and you will—you'll also see various gopher statues around the town. The largest statue is 3.7 metres tall and features an overall-clad gopher named Clem T. GoFur. You'll also notice that all the fire hydrants in town are painted to look like Clem's relatives. Go phigure!

Torrington is an hour northeast of Calgary. The Gopher Hole Museum is open daily from 10:00 AM to 5:00 PM from June 1 to September 30.

~ Big, Gargantuan & Ridiculously Oversized ~

The "World's Largest Snowman" (obviously not made of real snow) is located in Beardmore, Ontario, near Lake Nipigon. At 10.7 metres tall, it easily beats the one in Kenaston, Saskatchewan (south of Saskatoon), which also claims the title. The Beardmore snowman also comes with removable seasonal accessories: in summer, he sports sunglasses and a fishing pole; in winter, he's got a curling broom and a scarf. Snowmen are stylish to a fault!

THE ROOT CELLAR CAPITAL OF THE WORLD
ELLISTON, NEWFOUNDLAND

I didn't even know there was such a thing as the "Root Cellar Capital of the World," let alone that it would be in Newfoundland and that they'd actually tell people about it. But, in fact, in the year 2000, Elliston declared itself the "Root Cellar Capital of the World." And no one seems to be disputing that. I'm making a bit of fun here, but this little piece of weird is taken very seriously in Elliston, which in my books makes it that much weirder.

There are apparently 135 documented root cellars in Elliston, which makes it some sort of nexus of the root cellar universe. The oldest root cellar still in use today dates back to 1839.

So, just what is a root cellar? Root cellars originated before the time of electricity—in the dark times, I guess you could say. People built these structures to keep their vegetables from freezing over the winter or to keep them cool in summer. The cellars have also been known to house homemade alcoholic beverages.

The cellars were often dug into the sides of hills or built from the ground up using rocks and sod. The newer root cellars are, however, made of concrete. If you're ever in Newfoundland, the good folks of Elliston want you to come and see their proudest attractions, the root cellars! It's a world capital, remember?

You'll find Elliston on the Atlantic Ocean, not far from Bonavista.

THE SINGING SANDS
BASIN HEAD BEACH, PRINCE EDWARD ISLAND

Generally speaking, I prefer my sand to be silent…oh yeah, and inanimate. So, that's probably why I wouldn't visit Basin Head Beach near Souris on the eastern tip of PEI. The beach is beautiful—a golden sand paradise. But as you walk along that beach, you'll think someone's following you. That's because the sand sings—more accurately, it kind of squeaks.

Scientists aren't actually sure why the sand on some beaches whistles and sings, but the squeaking phenomenon is found where quartz sand is extremely well rounded and spherical. Other squeaking, whistling, singing and even barking sand beaches have been found in the north of Wales on the Scottish island of Eigg, at a few other places along the Atlantic Coast and on the island of Kauai in Hawaii.

So if you're looking for a quiet little paradise-like beach, you'll want to avoid those and the Singing Sands of PEI. The fiddle music in the area is pretty good, but rarely does it keep time with the squeaking beach. Different unions, I guess.

~ Big, Gargantuan & Ridiculously Oversized ~

Now, what kind of gift does one get for a Manitoba town? Giant fly swatter? Big can of polar bear repellent? Maybe a town-sized parka… All good ideas, but none of them would fly for the officers and men of the soon-to-be-closed Canadian Forces Base Gimli. In true flyboy fashion, they gave the town of Gimli one of their T-33 Silver Star jets. Apparently in the move, they ended up with a spare. The base closed in 1971, and the "T-Bird" was stuck on top of a concrete pillar at the south end of First Avenue. Colonel Jim Dunlop formally presented the T-33 to the town of Gimli on July 17, 1971. I wonder how he wrapped it?

THE IGLOO CHURCH
INUVIK, NORTHWEST TERRITORIES

Officially, it's called Our Lady of Victory Roman Catholic Church, but throughout the Arctic, it's simply known as the Igloo Church. And why is it called the Igloo Church? Well, it's a church that's shaped like an igloo. Duh!

Brother Maurice Larocque and Father Joseph Adam designed the Igloo Church in 1958. Using largely volunteer labour, it took two years to build the structure, which opened in 1960. The church is nearly 23 metres in diameter, circular and 21 metres tall. It's also topped by a dome with a cupola and cross.

And the big question—why is it shaped like an igloo? Largely to keep from melting the permafrost, which if it did melt would cause the building to shift. The Igloo Church was designed and built with a double shell and sits on a bowl of gravel that's set into the ground, which apparently overcomes the permafrost issue.

It's innovative, functional, worshipful and one of the most photographed structures in the Arctic! It's no inukshuk, but it's outstanding nonetheless.

Inuvik is 3298 kilometres north of Edmonton, Alberta. If you're heading that way, I'd suggest you go by plane.

DANCELAND
MANITOU BEACH, SASKATCHEWAN

A place called Danceland that's located at the edge of a Saskatchewan lake doesn't sound so strange. In fact, I went back and forth on whether to include this one or not. However, when I started talking to people about it, their expressions were full of puzzlement, and that's when I knew the place was definitely weird.

Danceland is known as the "Home of the World Famous Dance Floor Built on Horsehair." Horsehair, you say? I do.

When the place was built way back in 1928, the maple hardwood floor was laid atop two subfloors with 15-centimetre rolls of horsetail (horsehair) wrapped in burlap sandwiched in between. The 15-centimetre layer of horsehair allows the floor to give up to 4 centimetres and dancers to almost glide across the 465 m² dance floor. Danceland also has other advantages such as its arched roof, which gives it great acoustics.

When Danceland was built, there were three similar halls in North America. They've all since been demolished. Danceland, with its horsehair-cushioned floor, remains unique. And nothing, apparently, compares to it for dancing on!

Danceland is open year round and is located 113 kilometres southeast of Saskatoon in Watrous, Saskatchewan.

COCHIN LIGHTHOUSE
COCHIN, SASKATCHEWAN

The only lighthouse in Saskatchewan is located in Cochin. And, as one might likely predict of a land-locked province, the Cochin Lighthouse serves no real seafaring purpose. It overlooks both Cochin and Jackfish Lakes from a narrow isthmus between the two. It provides great views for tourists as well.

The Cochin Lighthouse sits atop Pirot Hill. More than 150 steps lead up the hill to the base of the lighthouse. The structure is almost 12 metres tall, painted white and octagonal in shape. The lighthouse also has the requisite rotating beacon that can be seen for miles around.

You'll find Cochin nestled amongst rolling hills and scenic lakes, just 30 kilometres north of North Battleford in, where else, north-central Saskatchewan.

HÔTEL DE GLACE
LAKE ST. JOSEPH, QUÉBEC

Each January, just 30 minutes west of Québec City, you can slip and slide into North America's only ice hotel. Open from January to April, the Hôtel de Glace is made entirely of ice (360 tonnes) and snow (11,000 tonnes) There are 34 rooms than can accommodate a total of 84 people each frigid night. If you do the math, that's a little more than two people per room. Clearly some icy Québecois fun is going on in the *chambres*.

The architecture of the hotel changes each year, as does the unique and original ice artwork and ice furniture found inside. The hotel's walls are over a metre thick, and the ceilings are 5.5 metres high, keeping the inside temperature hovering somewhere between a balmy –2 to –5°C. There's a bar, a dance club and a chapel included in the icy *pension* for those wishing to consume an icy cold beverage, boogie or get married.

Just in case you're wondering, the ice hotel does, in fact, also include bathroom facilities… Apparently they are heated, and we say thank gawd to that! I mean, can you imagine a midnight pee where you go "whee" because it's so icy?

~ Big, Gargantuan & Ridiculously Oversized ~

The "World's Largest Fiddle" used to be 7.3 metres tall in Cavendish, Prince Edward Island. The fiddle is still in Cavendish, but its "world's largest" status has been usurped by the 16.8-metre-tall fiddle in Sydney, Nova Scotia. "Big Ceilidh Fiddle," as it is officially known, is owned by the Sydney Ports Corporation and was built to capture the attention of visitors. As well, a 4-metre-high fiddle commemorates the great Don Messer in his hometown of Harvey, New Brunswick. Clearly the Maritimes aren't fiddling around with their big fiddles!

THE MYSTERIOUS

MYSTERY ROCKS
SASKATCHEWAN

About a 45-minute hike from Fort Walsh in Cypress Hills Interprovincial Park, there is an odd formation of rocks that has mystified folks and defied explanation. Giant rocks appear to be fitted together to form a kind of road or wall. But no one seems to be able to explain how the rocks got there. They may even have been there for thousands of years, which just adds to the mystery.

People, including scientists, have been debating the origin of the rocks, and theories range from a geological anomaly to an ancient civilization and even to alien or UFO construction. So far, no solid explanations have been found.

Some people think the rock formations have similarities to the mysterious underwater formation called the Bimini Road in the Bahamas or look somewhat like the giant interconnected rocks found at Machu Picchu in Peru. But again, how did the rocks get there? The mystery continues and is not likely to be solved anytime soon.

The rocks are actually located on private property, so if you want to see them you'll have to ask permission at Fort Walsh.

Cypress Hills Interprovincial Park is located in southwestern Saskatchewan, near the Montana border. The visitor centre is located in Val Marie, about 120 kilometres south of Swift Current.

THE HAMMER OF THOR
PAYNE RIVER, UNGAVA, QUÉBEC

In far northeastern Québec, just north of Payne Bay, there stands a 3.3-metre-tall obelisk that looks like a crude hammer. It was discovered in the 1960s, but has actually been there for longer than anyone in the area can remember.

The Inuit don't claim it as theirs. In fact, they say it predates them. Although there is no proof, the "Hammer of Thor," as it's been called, has been attributed to Europeans—the Norse, to be more specific. It's been held up as evidence of Viking occupation of the Ungava region 1000 years ago.

Others claim the Hammer of Thor could be Inuit in origin or possibly Scottish. The debate rages, but conclusive evidence is elusive. The Inuit continue doing their thing on the Ungava, and life goes on whether Thor's Hammer has a maker or not.

DEFINITELY ON THE VERGE OF BEING OFFENSIVE

THE LAND OF RAPE AND HONEY
TISDALE SASKATCHEWAN

Tisdale, Saskatchewan, is known as "The Land of Rape and Honey." No, it's not a slogan that celebrates a heinous act—though it sure sounds like it does! The town's slogan is actually in reference to the fact that the community produces large quantities of both rapeseed or "rape" (now known as canola) and about 10% of Canada's honey. And that's how they got the slogan "The Land of Rape and Honey."

I understand that the people of northeastern Saskatchewan are practical, straightforward and shoot from the hip, but what that slogan lacks in subtlety, it more than makes up for in its fresh-faced, naïve offensiveness!

~ Big, Gargantuan & Ridiculously Oversized ~

The town of Kimberley, BC, is the home of North America's largest free-standing cuckoo clock. The Rocky Mountain town was already known for its Bavarian theme when the clock was originally built back in 1972. Instead of a cuckoo bird popping out on the hour, Happy Hans, a strange and demonic (just kidding!) bearded figure yodels each hour. If you can't wait for the top of the hour, you can drop a quarter in the clock and Happy Hans will emerge a-yodelling. The clock and Happy Hans are located at the Platzl Mall downtown.

COVERT CIA FLIGHTS
ST. JOHN'S INTERNATIONAL AIRPORT, NEWFOUNDLAND

With growing concern in European countries about covert CIA flights spiriting unnamed and perhaps illegally kidnapped persons to covert internment camps and information retrieval sites, Canadians woke up in November 2005 to discover that our airports may be being used in similar ways.

Canadian press reports identified a 40-seat turboprop landing in St. John's, Newfoundland. It was a private plane registered to Devon Holding and Leasing Inc. of Lexington, North Carolina—a company that has been linked to the CIA. The turboprop flew in from Iceland, made a stop in St. John's, travelled to Manchester, New Hampshire, and then to its final destination, Johnston County Airport in Smithfield, North Carolina—an airport that is thought to be a centre for covert American air operations.

Clearly, there's definite proof about the flights and their alleged covert nature. There's also a lot of circumstantial evidence mounting. Only time will tell how offended Canadians will be at the idea that their airports are being used as a weird stopover for mysterious CIA flights. This is especially true in the light of the Maher Arar case and inquiry.

If I Can Celebrate There,
I Can Celebrate Anywhere

It's official!

*All the ballots are in, and the first annual winner of the
Provincial or Territorial Award of Distinction with
Regard to Short-Term Weirdness—aka Crazy Canadian
Festivals—is New Brunswick. That's right, that quiet
little Maritime gem; that beguiler of bilingualism; that
place sandwiched between Maine, Québec, PEI
and Nova Scotia.*

It's a winner!

*Why? Well, New Brunswick is home to festivals cele-
brating molluscs, Brussels sprouts, fiddleheads, giant
pumpkins, chocolate, dory boats and peat moss.
That is one eclectic mix!*

*Ontario may have albino woodchucks and squirrels of
both the white and black variety; Saskatchewan may* ☞

have the Duck Derby and Chicken Chariot Races. Hey, Newfoundland even has the "Root Cellar Capital of Canada." But New Brunswick's mix of food, fun and frolic puts it way ahead of the rest of us.

So, let's hoist one on high for New Brunswick and proclaim: Spem reduxit *("Hope was restored")—that's the provincial motto, don't ya know!*

FESTIVAL PROVINCIAL DE LA TOURBE
LAMÈQUE, NEW BRUNSWICK

Lamèque lies on the tip of New Brunswick's Acadian Peninsula. It's a small community of about 1600 people. The area has an eco-park nearby, some pretty good campgrounds and great scenery. None of this makes Lamèque particularly weird. What does make Lamèque, at least in the short term, particularly weird is the Festival provincial de la tourbe.

And I say, where better to have the Festival provincial de la tourbe than Lamèque, New Brunswick. Since Lamèque is the province's capital de la tourbe. So, just what is the Festival provincial de la tourbe? It's a peat moss festival, of course. *Mon dieu!*

Lamèque lies at the very northeastern tip of New Brunswick, and its moist climate and flat terrain make it perfect for growing peat moss. In fact, New Brunswick is the second largest world exporter of the moss known as peat. During the festival, you can visit the peatlands, wave to the peat, act like peat and even pet the peat. I wonder how many locals are named Peat? Or Pete?

Apparently the locals take their harvest celebrations seriously. A highlight of the festival is the way people decorate their homes, offices and harvesting areas with bales of peat. I'm imagining giant doilies made of peat moss, or perhaps a peat moss dragon, or even a peat-like mollusc named Peat! But let's hope the Lamèque decorators don't do what my cousin Bill does with his Christmas lights. I mean, they're up all year round. I bet if you do that with peat, it starts to get a bit musty…for peat's sake!

The festival takes place each July.

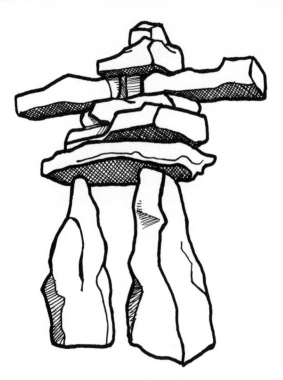

~ Big, Gargantuan & Ridiculously Oversized ~

Inukshuks are quickly becoming the most ubiquitous symbol of Canada. They may soon rival long-heralded symbols such as the moose, beaver and maple leaf. Perhaps there should be a contest, or even a cartoon reality show in which Inukshuk, Moose, Beaver and Maple Leaf duke it out in goofy, pointless contests with the winner becoming Canada's official symbol, sign and mascot…or maybe not. However, inukshuks are everywhere. Two—a male and a female, if there is such a thing—in Newmarket, Ontario; a squat-looking one in Marmora, Ontario; an extremely fat one in Collingwood, Ontario; a very large one in Vancouver, BC; a tall, sinewy one in Hay River in the Northwest Territories; and the grand-daddy of them all, a very tall one at Rankin Inlet, Nunavut. The Rankin Inlet one is large enough, in fact, for an average-height man to stand comfortably between its legs. That photo-op alone has got to be worth the trek to Rankin Inlet!

FESTIVAL DES CHOUX
DE BRUXELLES
ROGERSVILLE, NEW BRUNSWICK

Rogersville is a community of about 1300 people located 100 kilometres north of Moncton and 35 kilometres south of Miramichi. According to the region's tourism materials, it offers guests "a panoply of events, historical sites to visit, plus great places to stay and eat." A panoply, huh? Read on… You can relax at Parc Mille Pas (Park of 1000 Footsteps), visit the Trappist Fathers 5 kilometres north of the town or head to the town in the summer for its big and weird festival celebrating the Brussels sprout.

Yuck!

What in gawd's name would make anyone, anywhere, anytime celebrate Brussels sprouts? I apologize to the good people of Rogersville, but this is one vegetable-like substance that I just cannot abide! I know they're supposed to be full of cancer-fighting vitamins, but the only thing I can think of doing with them is packing them into a blunderbuss and firing them at the enemy coming over the hill. This, apparently, is not one of the activities at the Festival des choux de Bruxelles.

Festival activities include breakfasts and barbecues. It just gets better and better! Sprouts on the barbecue and for breakfast! I'll bet there's some form of sprout shake involved. Perhaps they could contact the good folks of Lamèque (see previous weird place) and top it all off by adding a fashion show in which all the dresses include a sprout motif with a peat fringe!

Other activities at the sprout festival include a mini-sprout pageant (I'm seeing a portly version of the Jolly Green Giant), a treasure hunt (oh, I can't wait to line up to find the golden sprout), sprout dances, sprout bingo, sprout bike and car rallies, a sprout strongman competition and the always popular sprout parade.

What about a good tossing event? You know what I mean, like in the village of Buñol in Spain, where they pelt each other with ripe tomatoes. Think about it! The festival would build up to the great sprout rout, where teams grab handfuls of the tiny cabbage-like chokers and whip them at each other until everyone is black and blue from the green... And then I never have to taste another one of them in my life.

It's starting to sound a little more fun, don't ya think?

The Festival des choux de Bruxelles takes place annually during the last week of July.

~ Big, Gargantuan & Ridiculously Oversized ~

Sundial Folly is located at the foot of York Street in Harbour Square Park West in Toronto and is oft used as a meeting place or point of reference. People call it "that cracked egg thing," the "concrete ball" or "that round thing over there." It's made up of a ramp leading into a 2.7-metre-diameter hollow concrete sphere with a 1-metre piece removed from bottom to top on the harbour side. This harbour-side cut allows sunlight into the sphere and frames a view of the inner harbour and the Toronto Islands. There is also a cascading wall of water beside the orb and a circulating pool beside and inside it. The whole thing kind of looks like Mork from Ork just landed and his egg ship is sinking into the harbour because he forgot to shut the door. No, really. Picture it. Sundial Folly was unveiled in 1995 and was the first project of two talented and enterprising architecture grads fresh out of the University of Waterloo. Their winning design beat out 144 other proposals, some of them from well-known and established artists. That's got to hurt! The unique sculpture has been used for many things, including a homeless shelter, peeing hut, teenage drinking place and, my absolute favourite, the stage for a 1999 performance piece featuring a dancer, a mezzo-soprano and musicians playing clarinet and hurdy-gurdy. Folly, indeed!

FESTIVAL DES MOLLUSQUES
BOUCTOUCHE, NEW BRUNSWICK

The Mi'kmaq originally called the New Brunswick town of Bouctouche "Chebooktoosk," which meant "big little harbour." The town dates back to 1785, when François and Charlitte LeBlanc carved a cross in a tall pine tree, setting the symbolic stage for making the banks of the Chebooktoosk their home. It's large for a small port, but too small to be a large one—the Mi'kmaq clearly knew what they were talking about. The town is located where the Bouctouche River empties into the Northumberland Strait. It's noted for its silken shores, as the birthplace of that giant of East Coast business, K.C. Irving, and for the Festival des mollusques.

That's right, a festival of molluscs. A festival celebrating all that is mollusc, mollusc-like and mollusc to be.

And for the $250 prize: What is a mollusc? Anyone?

Answer: According to the Oxford dictionary, molluscs are any invertebrate of the phylum Mollusca, having a soft body and usually a hard shell… So, does that help? What we're talking about here is slugs, snails, oysters, mussels, clams, scallops, squid and octopi.

Every July, the tiny village of Bouctouche sees an influx of visitors, who are basically there to sample and devour the great bounty of molluscs that New Brunswick has to offer. In 2006, the 31st anniversary of the festival will include lobster boils, beer gardens, races, fireworks, a really big parade and, of course, the festival's highlight, the Pageant des guidounes. *Guidounes* is, of course, a slang word in French for "tramps," so I suspect the "Pageant of Tramps" is some weird and wild thing to see! Other highlights include a strongman competition, bluegrass music and country fiddlers.

You can get a sampling of true Acadian cuisine with the infamous *poutine râpée*, which is, of course, grated, raw and mashed potatoes wrapped around fresh pork. Not terribly mollusc-related, but how many molluscs can one devour? No really, how many? Anyone have an estimate?

The Festival des mollusques takes place in mid-July. Bouctouche is halfway between Shediac and Miramichi along Route 11 on New Brunswick's beautiful and scenic East Coast.

~ Big, Gargantuan & Ridiculously Oversized ~

As if a town having the name Goobies, Newfoundland, isn't enough of a tourist draw, in front of a local Irving Big Stop Gas station stands a giant moose named Morris. Presiding over the number 210 intersection, Morris stands 3.5 metres tall and is 3 metres long. He was built as a tourist attraction and to remind people to be mindful of moose while driving. Fatalities from moose-car-people encounters are more than a little common in these parts.

THE FIDDLEHEAD FESTIVAL
FREDERICTON, NEW BRUNSWICK

Let's face it, capital cities in every province are a bit off-kilter. They have their own way of doing things. They dance to their own drummer, to put a clichéd, yet positive spin on it. Or at least that's the take if you're someone not living in a capital city. So why should New Brunswick's capital, Fredericton, be any different? Well…it's not.

Fredericton has been home to notorious American traitor Benedict Arnold, sports a "little nude dude" atop its City Hall Fountain and was the place where the "railway flanger" was invented. That's a sort of a snowplow-clearing device for tracks.

But in my mind, the weirdest aspect of Fredericton is its middle of May festival celebrating the unassuming little fiddlehead…That's right! Each year, the St. Mary's First Nation celebrates the fiddlehead. Fiddleheads, you know, are those highly perishable young fronds of the ostrich fern. This is all new to me! I've never had one! Didn't even know what they looked like before I did my research. But apparently the tightly curled green shoots are picked before their leaves unfurl. I'm from the city, so I have no idea what all of this means.

Anyway, the fiddlehead is a symbol of the Wolastoqiyik along the St. John River. The Fiddlehead Festival includes a whole lot of fiddlehead eating, a fiddlehead dance, great moments in fiddlehead history and fiddlehead stories. Like the one about the two fiddleheads who go into a bar and pick a fight with a Brussels sprout, a mollusc and some peat…

THE WIARTON WILLIE FESTIVAL
WIARTON, ONTARIO

Wiarton is a small and more than pleasant town located on an inlet of Georgian Bay at the southern end of Ontario's Bruce Peninsula. The town has a population of about 2300 and was incorporated as a village in 1880. The community originally thrived on the success of its lumber industry, but is now known for great area beaches and tourism.

And in this quaint little slice of Canadiana, a strange little annual event takes place. In the dead of winter, a guy dressed to the nines and standing next to another guy in a white groundhog costume reaches into the town-sponsored den of the famous White Woodchuck, Wiarton Willie, pulls Willie from his snug-as-a-bug-in-a-rug den, hoists him high into the air and hopes the pink-eyed little albino can give some indication as to whether he sees his shadow or not. I don't know—I think this annual ritual definitely falls under the "weird" heading…way weird!

Wiarton may be the location of the granddaddy of all weird Canadian festivals—the Wiarton Willie Festival—or as it is known to most of us in North America, Groundhog Day (February 2). Wiarton is 240 kilometres northwest of Toronto, which puts it in a good position for people from southern Ontario to flock there for the annual event. Ka-ching!

They've been celebrating Groundhog Day in Wiarton since 1956. Early groundhog prognosticators were named Grundoon, Sandoon and Muldoon, but were rather ordinary as groundhogs go.

Upon the arrival of the first Wiarton Willy in the 1980s, things really heated up for this weird festival. The first Wiarton Willie, as well as his successors, have all been albino groundhogs. That's right—they have white fur and pink eyes and can't see too well, which is interesting considering that W.W.'s main job is to look for his shadow once a year. Oh, the stress of it all! Sounds like a government job.

It may actually be a bit strenuous, considering that the first Wiarton Willie died tragically just before the festival in 1999. W.W. number one was replaced that year by a stuffed, reasonable facsimile of himself. Since then, they've kept two Wiarton Willies on hand just in case a tragedy befalls one of them.

The Wiarton Willie Festival actually runs for two weeks and includes hockey tournaments, dances, parades, snooker tournaments, Monte Carlo night, a fish fry and a circus.

The big question? How accurate is Wiarton Willie in his predictions of a truncated winter? Well, about the same as all the groundhog psychics. In general, groundhogs are correct less than 40% of the time. Neither America's Punxsutawney

Phil, Manitoba's Brandon Bob, Alberta's Balzac Billy or Nova Scotia's Shubenacadie Sam do any better. In 2006, Wiarton celebrated the 50th anniversary of its white-woodchuck-centred festival. I'll bet a good time was had by all!

~ Big, Gargantuan & Ridiculously Oversized ~

The self-proclaimed "Sunflower Capital of Canada," Altona, Manitoba, is also the home of the "World's Largest Painting on an Easel." Not surprisingly, the painting is a replica of one of Vincent Van Gogh's sunflower paintings. The easel is 25 metres tall, and the reproduction painting is 7 metres wide by 10 metres tall. This was the first completed giant easel erected as part of the Van Gogh Project. The intent of the project is to erect similar giant replicas all over the world. The second was erected in Emerald, Australia. A third is being constructed in Goodland, Kansas, and others are being discussed for South Africa and Japan.

CHICKEN CHARIOT RACES
WYNYARD, SASKATCHEWAN

Wynyard is the self-proclaimed "Chicken Capital of Western Canada." I guess *Harrowsmith* magazine doesn't have a category for this, so the town had to proclaim it for itself. It's also because the town's processing plant is known for raising and doing other things to a whole heck of a lot of chickens. The town proper has a population of fewer than 2000 people and is located 150 kilometres west of Yorkton, Saskatchewan. Wynyard was first settled by Icelanders and is named for the English family of the wife of a railroad official. She must have been something to have her family's name on the town and not his. It's a quiet town full of typically hard-working Saskatchewanites who once a year blow the lid off, get a little funky and do some odd, odd things to chickens...other than sell them to Colonel Sanders.

Each June, the Wynyard Carnival plays host to the annual Chicken Chariot Race. I have to say, I think this one has to be seen to be believed.

I chatted with a former Kinsmen (the Wynyard Kinsmen run the event) named Harold Wasylenka. He described the whole chicken-lickin' good proceedings for me. There are four lanes per heat, all separated by Plexiglas runners. A single chicken pulls each chariot. I asked if chickens need training to pull chariots. Harold told me that some people think the chickens need training. However, he says, if you attach something to the back of a chicken, it wants to run! Practical advice from a Saskatchewan native! Chickens, so I've been told, aren't that bright. And they are easily frightened. The record for the fastest race is somewhere in the vicinity of 20 seconds. And with a course length of about 15 metres, the poultry is flying like s*** through a goose.

DUCK DERBY
LUMSDEN, SASKATCHEWAN

Lumsden is a town of about 1600 people situated just 30 kilometres northwest of Regina, Saskatchewan. The town has a lot to offer, including an arena, a petting zoo and the nearby Last Mountain Provincial Park, which recreates a former 19th-century fur-trading post. In 2002, *Harrowsmith Country Life* magazine named Lumsden one of Canada's top 10 prettiest towns. In 2003, the same magazine named Lumsden Saskatchewan's prettiest town. Seems this pretty little town is getting a little greedy with the *Harrowsmith* accolades, don't ya think? But that may just be my jealousy talking, since I'm originally from Hamilton.

But with all this prettiness, there must be something else going on—something, odd, unusual or perhaps even a bit weird? Yeah, I'd call the annual Duck Derby weird!

And just what the heck is a Duck Derby? Well, unlike Saskatchewan's equally famous Wynyard Chicken Chariot Races, the Lumsden Duck Derby does not involve actual animals. Well, not living, breathing animals, anyhow. Basically it involves thousands of rubber duckies drifting down a kilometre-long course on the Qu'Appelle River. Say what?

Okay, each year, veteran "Duckettes" (people dressed up as duck mascots) sell $5 tickets. Each ticket buys a rubber ducky for the race. On race day, a parade assembles that each year resembles less and less a race to the post—like with the Kentucky Derby.

Following the parade, everyone gathers at the river's edge. A large metal cage is hoisted into the air, and then the cage is opened and thousands of ducks spill out. The ducks race, or more accurately, float really slowly, to the finish line. The first 10 ducks to cross the line are the winners, and each corresponding sponsor wins a prize. Races have ended in less than 50 minutes. However, they've also taken as along as five hours.

The whole fun and ridiculous derby was started to help pay for the town's arena $1.5 million arena. That's been paid off since 1998, so now the funds go to other fun projects. A duck derby wins the day. Charity casinos indeed!

The Duck Derby takes place each year on Labour Day.

YUKON RIVER BATHTUB RACE
YUKON RIVER, WHITEHORSE TO DAWSON, YUKON

So what can one say about the Yukon River? It's definitely long—2300 miles and tied with the Mississippi/Missouri as the second-longest river in North America. Only the Mackenzie is longer. Most of the river lies in Alaska and is navigable by ships from Whitehorse to the Bering Sea, though the Dawson to Whitehorse part is only navigable by smaller ships. The river is frozen over for more than six months of the year, leaving little time for wet and wild fun and frolic. Which brings us to the weird part.

The annual Yukon River Bathtub Race has been dubbed the longest and toughest bathtub race in the world. At 782 kilometres, the race traverses the Yukon River from Whitehorse to Dawson City in mid-May. The race celebrates its 15th anniversary in 2006.

Competitors are called tubbers. Some of the craft less resemble bathtubs than small speedboats, though according to the official rules, each craft must conform to the general shape and design of an old-style edge bathtub.

The promotional material for the 12th annual race explains the race's history this way: "Once upon a time, a very bored northern man looked upon his equally bored northern wife and said, 'Let's say we get all the boys together and race bathtubs down the Yukon River!?!?…' She replied, 'Whatever…'"

The race starts in Whitehorse, apparently "at the crack of 9(ish) and sends a dozen or so of the world's most adventurous souls down the Yukon River in 5-foot x 3-foot bathtubs!" Or so says the web site for the race. On the first day, tubbers traverse the Five Finger Rapids, and their day ends in McCabe Creek with a mandatory shower and barbecue. No word on whether the shower and barbeque come as a combo unit.

The second day of the competition sees the tubbers completing their trek and crossing the soggy finish line in Dawson City. In Dawson, tubbers are cheered on by crowds, copious drinks are served and thousands of dollars in prizes are awarded. The first-ever race took 33 hours to complete. Now it's a bit shorter, but no less fun!

THE GREAT KLONDIKE INTERNATIONAL OUTHOUSE RACE
DAWSON, YUKON

Dawson lies on the bank of the Yukon River near where it meets the Klondike. Formerly known as Dawson City, the community grew out of a marshy swamp after the discovery of gold in Bonanza Creek in 1896. It became the largest city in Canada west of Winnipeg in a scant two years, with 40,000 inhabitants. The town was founded by a former prospector named Joe Ladue, who figured out that merchants prospered more in gold camps than did prospectors. The town was the capital of Yukon from 1898 to 1952, when Whitehorse got the nod. Since then the population has declined, but the settlement still retains a hardcore citizenry of about 2000 people. And these hardcore citizens are known for their sense of fun, their love of laughter and an odd little event.

Each Labour Day, the good folks of Dawson embark on a tradition of merriment, frolic and…ummmmm, privy-riding.

Competitors are tasked with building their own outhouse, or renting one from the Klondike Visitors Association. Next, five-person teams decorate their private privies to perfection, and then race the outhouses around a 3-kilometre course. Four of the team members are involved in the pushing. Of the outhouse, that is. The fifth member of the team is the designated sitter. That's right—sitter! The pushers carry or push the privies up and down hills, through gravel and across paved surfaces, all in the hope of winning a fortune in toilet paper. Actually, there are cash prizes. Not sure about the toilet paper.

Some past innovations in the decorating challenge have included: "The Whizzer of Oz" with Dorothy, Toto and the rest of the gang, and four prison guards pushing an O.J. Simpson look-alike in "Canned Juice." Get it? (O.J. Simpson's nickname used to be Juice.) And when you're a prisoner, you're often said to be in the "can," which is also a term used to describe an outhouse. These people are fun!

~ Big, Gargantuan & Ridiculously Oversized ~

An hour east of Edmonton, on the Yellowhead Highway, you'll discover the town of Vegreville, Alberta. Vegreville is famous for having the "World's Largest Pysanka." A pysanka is, of course, the Ukrainian word for Easter egg. And a large percentage of the population in Vegreville is descended from Ukrainian immigrants. So why not build the world's largest pysanka in 1974 to commemorate the 100th anniversary of the Royal Canadian Mounted Police? Why not, indeed? And why not mount a Mountie atop the egg? Because it's just silly, that's why…and rude! The good people of Vegreville did not add the Mountie, but they did build the pysanka for the RCMP centennial. The giant pysanka is not just famous for being big—though it is 7 metres long and 5.5 metres in diameter and stands 9.4 metres tall from base to top. It's famous also for its beauty and for achieving nine mathematical, architectural and engineering firsts. I won't bore you with those, but suffice it to say a computer scientist from the University of Utah—Ronald Resch—was brought in to design the pysanka and did so by being the first person to do a computer model of an egg. The pysanka rests on a rather heavy base that allows it to turn in the wind like a weather vane. Queen Elizabeth II and the Duke of Edinburgh visited the pysanka on their royal visit in 1978. Prince Philip was heard to say: "I'd like to see the blood sausage that goes with that, eh Liz!" Just kidding. But it does sound like something he'd say, eh?

SNOWKING WINTER FESTIVAL
YELLOWKNIFE, NORTHWEST TERRITORIES

I think when most people in Canada think of Yellowknife they think of cold…of snow…and of ice… Most of us also know that Yellowknife is the capital of the Northwest Territories and the only city in the territory with more than 19,000 residents. Geographically speaking, Yellowknife is situated on the north shore of Great Slave Lake. Something many people may not know is that Yellowknife got its name from the copper knives used by First Nations people who moved into the area in the 1800s. But let's get back to the cold and the ice and the weirdly long winter.

SnowKing says: "Winter is not weird." Okay, but it is damn cold, especially on the ice of Great Slave Lake. But each year for "ought 10 or more" (grizzled 1890s prospector talk for "about 10 or more"), his Majesty SnowKing has built a castle on the ice of Great Slave Lake and celebrated the season in wacky fashion, which makes it all a bit weird, unique, interesting, odd and fun! They start building SnowKing's castle in December or January, even though the festival doesn't start until March. Must be some castle!

I asked SnowKing to give me some details about his castle, but he wasn't giving anything away. "How the castle is built must be a guarded secret, and you can't handle the responsibility until you've spent time in the quarry cutting blocks," his Majesty proclaimed. For more details, SnowKing said I had to convince my publisher to shell out for a return air ticket and hotel for a week so I could be on "ground zero," learning at the elbow of the master—that would be SnowKing. Actually, the whole thing sounds like a hoot, so who knows, I may just show up this year. I mean, if it's good enough for Rick Mercer and the *Monday Report*?

SnowKing's festival includes events like the Royal Puppet Theatre, the annual Peter Gzowski Invitational Golf Tournament, SnowKing's Royal Ball (with orbs, sceptres and ladies-in-parkas-in-waiting, no doubt) and the Frozen Dog Film Festival, which I hope is not a film festival chronicling the freezing of a dog. SnowKing is always looking for sponsors and accepting bookings for the Royal Icy SnowKing Chapel. Indeed, winter is not weird. But I have to say I think SnowKing is a bit. And good for him!

~ Big, Gargantuan & Ridiculously Oversized ~

It's a Bigfoot! It's an ape! It's my uncle Mel in a diaper smoking a cigar?! Well, the pictures of this roadside Sasquatch in Vermilion Bay, Ontario (west of Dryden), could be any of the above. I have no idea who the artist was, and I'm betting he wants to keep it that way. The—for the sake of argument, we'll call it "Bigfoot"— Bigfoot is 5.5 metres tall and sits on the Trans-Canada Highway in front of a gas station. And he looks angry, my friends! His arms are outstretched, and his thumbs reach into the sky. That's why some people think he's hitchhiking. I personally think his hands form a rude gesture, but he's a Bigfoot and has gotten the fingers mixed up. There is apparently a speaker inside the statue that allows the gas station's owners to mess with people's heads by having Bigfoot talk to them. Oh yeah, and I'll bet they're all fooled into thinking the Bigfoot mutant is real!

A Crater, a Ring
or a Glowing Orb

Some of the weirdest places we've ever encountered are, alas, no longer with us. They are relegated to pictures and memories and remembrances of better times. (Cue the violins.)

However, their impact on the weirdness that is Canada is not forgotten. And speaking of forgotten, we mustn't forget those places of folklore, myth and delusion that never were, that might have been or that perhaps were placed on a different plane of existence. Read on...

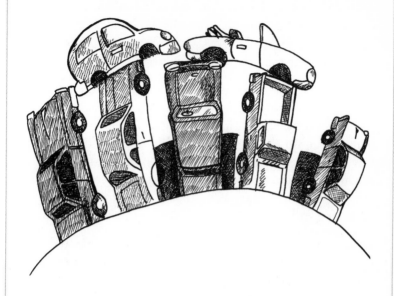

AUTOHENGE
OSHAWA, ONTARIO

Like the dawn of a new age, Autohenge rose on the grassy knoll of a farmer's field one morning back in 1986. It was conceived and built by a then little-known artist, environmentalist and true original, Bill Lishman. A farmer's field north of Oshawa was the setting for the full-scale replica of the infamous Salisbury Plain monument, except that it was built out of partially crushed cars as opposed to the original's sarsen and bluestones.

Chrysler Canada paid for the monument and used it in commercials to illustrate the fate of their rivals' cars. The sculptor used old cars, placed them vertically and crushed them slightly to create the familiar circular ring of Stonehenge. He then used more cars and capped some of the others to create a full-sized copy that included the post and lintel arrangement.

Autohenge existed for five years and attracted tourists from around the world. According to Bill Lishman, an extraordinary number of people experienced a profound sense of déjà vu while visiting Autohenge. Lishman says it happened to him the day they completed the sculpture.

On that same afternoon in 1986 when the structure was completed, Lishman remembers there was an impending electrical storm. He says he looked up at one moment to see that the hair on all four of the people working on the site was "standing straight out like dandelions gone to seed." Frightened by the sight, Lishman and his workers hightailed it out of there in a hurry. A neighbour later reported seeing a lightening strike within Autohenge's ring that very afternoon.

Sadly, Autohenge was dismantled in the early 1990s, and nothing is left except a subtle ring that sometimes shows in the crops that are grown on the knoll. The farmer who owned the land became worried about liability, and according to Bill Lishman: "Autohenge fell to the fear of those dark minions of Satan who might arrange blame on him for some perceived happening." Translation—it had become the site for moonlit teenage druid events, a spot where teenager girls sacrificed their virginity by night and others could supplement their incomes by day picking up empty beer bottles.

Bill Lishman went on to create an ice version of Stonehenge called Icehenge on Lake Scugog and many other sculptures, as well as an underground dwelling.

~ Big, Gargantuan & Ridiculously Oversized ~

The "World's Largest Dinosaur" stands very proud and very tall in Drumheller, Alberta. He's 25 metres tall and 46 metres long from head to tail. An actual T-rex only stood 4.5 metres tall and 12 metres long. Dino 2000, as the T-rex project is called, was built as part of the millennium celebrations. And this isn't just another dinosaur to be viewed from a distance. This one has 106 stairs inside that lead from just behind its right leg up into its mouth and onto a viewing platform. And what an experience it must be for brave tourists who get an insider's view of what it would be like to be one of those human hors d'oeuvres from the *Jurassic Park* films. Family-friendly fun!

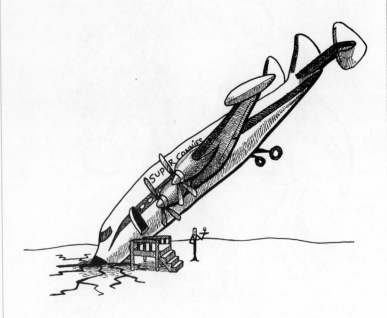

SUPER CONNIE'S AIRPLANE BAR
MISSISSAUGA, ONTARIO

What a concept! You take a beloved old passenger plane, anchor it to the ground, build wooden steps up to it fore and aft, and serve drinks to people inside it. If this isn't the height of kitsch, I don't know what is. And that's what they did at Toronto's Pearson Airport.

The plane in question is a Lockheed Super Constellation, and these planes are beyond beloved. Four propellers, black nose, three rudders...sleek mid-century design. This one previously flew with Trans Canada Airlines (TCA), the forerunner of Air Canada, and is apparently the last of TCA's Super Connies. Howard Hughes more or less designed this plane for TWA, where he was the controlling shareholder from

1939 to 1966. Most of the world's major airlines flew these planes in the 1940s and 1950s. They were also known as Starliners.

URGENT UPDATE: It looks as though Super Connie's Airplane Bar will never fly again as either a bar or a plane or as a Canadian-owned piece of aviation history. At press time, Super Connie's was being dismantled and prepared for shipment to its new owner, the Museum of Flight in Seattle, Washington. Air Canada has promised to paint the Super Connie in its original TCA colours, but many people involved in Canadian aviation are crying foul and hoping the federal government will cancel the sale by not granting an export permit. These people think the last Canadian Super Connie should remain Canadian.

However, whether it stays or goes, the airplane bar concept seems to be sunk. And barring a surprising turn of events, you'll have to visit the United States to see Canada's last Super Connie...

Run quickly if you want to see the Super Connie. Last time I checked, it was in pieces at the intersection of Derry Road East and Torbram Road in Mississauga. Who knows—with enough public outcry (hint, hint), the bar may fly again on Canadian soil...or the plane may bar again!

ESTOTILAND

Estotiland—a strange and wonderful place inhabited by people of European descent who have their own language, Latin books (that they don't know how to read), cities and the requisite New World pile of gold. The island became known in 1558, with the publication of a book and map of the voyages and discoveries of the Venetian brothers Antonio and Nicolo Zeno. The fabled—and lost or missing or never was—island of Estotiland has been pinpointed as being either Nova Scotia or Labrador. That's quite the pinpointing, don't you think! It gets better. The official Zeno documents and map describe Estotiland as being 1600 kilometres west of Frisland. Which is? Well, I guess as Canadians, we should be happy we've been included in the tall, Old World tales of lands that never were.

~ Big, Gargantuan & Ridiculously Oversized ~

"The Village of Glendon would like to welcome you to the home of the World's Largest Pyrogy, which is situated in Pyrogy Park just off Pyrogy Drive." So says the web site for the town of Glendon, Alberta—clearly a proud, proud pyrogy place! The large pyrogy in question is actually hanging off a giant fork stuck in the ground. The community is proud of its Ukrainian heritage, so what could be more appropriate as a tourist attraction than a giant, filled, dumpling-like thing that's an Eastern European staple? And the pyrogy has been worth its weight (2722 kilograms) in publicity gold! Newspapers, magazines and CNN have run stories about the Alberta town with the 8.2-metre-tall pyrogy. Beat that, Mount Rushmore!

MYSTERIOUS
TROPICAL VALLEY AND FORESTS
NAHANNI NATIONAL PARK,
NORTHWEST TERRITORIES

Remember that 1970s movie with Doug McClure, where he's among a group of Brits that are captured by a German U-boat. You know, the one where they end up in the Arctic and suddenly discover a tropical valley with dinosaurs and cavemen? Well, since time immemorial, there have been whispers, peeps and crazy legends about just such a tropical oasis in Canada's North. Parks Canada suggests that the most likely spot for such a place is at Kraus Hotsprings in Nahanni National Park in the Northwest Territories. The park is located along the South Nahanni River and a ways north of Fort Nelson, BC. Hang on a second! Kraus is a German name, and that 1970s film, *The Land that Time Forgot*, had Germans and their U-boat running roughshod over just such a valley... Coincidence? I think not!

Kraus Hotsprings is made up of two thermal hotsprings that spout water at 35°C, thus creating a paradise of lush green fields, tropical forests and dinosaurs. Parks Canada won't confirm either the green fields or the tropical forests, and they won't even talk to me about dinosaurs, but I know they're there. All they'll say is that the hotsprings smell of rotten eggs because of sulphur. And by the way, the Kraus Hotsprings are accessible only by boat, plane or on foot. This last piece of information begs the question: Just what is Parks Canada trying to keep secret?

~ Big, Gargantuan & Ridiculously Oversized ~

A potato that is 4.3 metres tall and 2.1 metres in diameter stands at the entrance to the Potato Museum in O'Leary, Prince Edward Island. The giant potato is made of fibreglass and is of the russet variety. Not to be outdone, the town of Vauxhall, Alberta, is known as the "Potato Capital of the West"—I assume they mean western Canada and not the Western Hemisphere. But in the tradition of great potato-growing regions, Sammy and Samantha Spud greet all visitors at the town's entrance with a sign that hangs between them. It appropriately reads: "Welcome to Vauxhall, Potato Capital of the West."

IT'S NOT OVER!

All good things must come to an end…or so they say. Although who "they" are is usually a mystery, in this case it is, in fact, my publisher. And so, it is with mixed emotions—perhaps cramps from sitting at this desk for so many weeks—that I bid a fond farewell to *Weird Canadian Places*.

The most disappointing thing about writing this book is that I had to omit literally thousands of weird things. There is only so much room and so few trees (for paper) since they grow so slowly. Damn them!

And if you've got suggestions, nominations or comments about what you've read, we'd love to hear from you, so write to us at bluebikebooks@yahoo.ca.

And go forth with this thought in mind: Everything is weird to someone!

ABOUT THE AUTHOR

Dan de Figueiredo

Dan de Figueiredo has been a journalist, television writer, filmmaker and playwright. His love for words began when his aunt and uncle gave him a copy of *Robinson Crusoe*, and he has never looked back. After earning his BA in political science at McMaster, followed by a BAA in journalism from Ryerson, Dan worked on the Canadian edition of *Who Wants to Be a Millionaire*, *Reach for the Top*, numerous television and theatre productions and several independent films. He is currently a freelance television writer, producer and researcher.